A GIFT FOR YOU

I hope you enjoy *Wising Up, Life Without Regrets.* Conceivably, you will gain insight and information that will assist you in your life.

If you know someone(s) who might benefit from the book, please consider purchasing one or more copies to give away. Thank you. **ISBN: 1-4184-1512-X**

List Price: $14.95

Books can be purchased at discount distributors:

www.wisinguphalmilton.com

www.authorhouse.com or call: 1-800/937-0152

www.amazon.com or other online sellers.

Also Available From: Your Favorite bookstore.

To Lauren & Jim
Your Wonderful!
Your presence is a blessing to all.
May your path be joyful as you become more wise ♡
Hal Milton 8/29/07

Wising Up

Life Without Regrets

by

Hal Milton

First published by AuthorHouse 07/07/04

ISBN: 1-4184-1511-1 (e-book)
ISBN: 1-4184-1512-X (Paperback)

Library of Congress Control Number: 2004091283

This book is printed on acid free paper.

Printed in the United States of America
Bloomington, IN

PRAISE FOR *WISING UP, LIFE WITHOUT REGRETS*

"*Wising Up* is a psychospiritual wake-up call to any of us who are getting older. It's a wonderful blend of personal sharing and spiritual wisdom that inspires us to continue to grow throughout all our years."

Rachel Harris, PhD
Psychologist, author *20-Minute Retreats* and
co-author *Children Learn What They Live* and
Teenagers Learn What They Live

"Hal Milton takes you on a journey through Eldering possibilities. He opens many gates to aging with awareness."

Rabbi Zalman Schachter-Shalomi
Author *From Age-ing to Sage-ing* and others.
Founder, the nondemoninational Spiritual
Eldering Institute.

"Science has given us longevity, but has not taught us to fulfill longevity's potential . . . Hal Milton has been many things, ranging from sports coach through body therapist to minister, and now he brings it all together in this book—along with his personal experiences of ageing. It will be of interest because he is not only gifted but an excellent human being and a sincere seeker."

Claudio Naranjo, M.D.

Author *Character and Neurosis*, *The Healing Journey*, *The One Quest*, and others. Fulbright Scholar and Guggenheim Fellow.

"*Wising Up* is a 'must read' for all those wanting to bring consciousness to the process of aging. It is a rich tapestry of myth, stories, science, and the author's personal experiences woven together with deep wisdom and practical spirituality. This book truly shows us how to grow wiser as we grow older."

Rev. Robert Brumet

Chairman, Pastoral Studies, Unity Institute.
author *Finding Yourself in Transition* and *The Quest for Wholeness.*

AUTHOR'S NOTE

Wising Up is for everybody: the middle-aged person, the aging boomer, and those of any age who are interested in *Wising Up* and living more consciously. Those who have met previously set goals, yet still feel that "something is missing," will find solutions here – through identification with stories and the suggested activities at the end of each chapter.

The number of spiritual and self-help books currently available is testament to the fact that many feel unfulfilled and that something in us needs to be fixed before we can be truly happy. Too often, we have allowed ourselves to be cubbyholed in our own minds by what we do for a living, what we have accomplished, or even by our failures. As "human doings" rather than human beings, we have become spiritually disconnected. Instead of expanding our lives and our awareness, we may have narrowed our views until we find ourselves living one-dimensional lives.

After over forty years of combined experience in teaching, creating, and facilitating workshops, I realized that our culture's focus is primarily on recreation and prolonging life, rather than the quality of that life. I concluded from my work and own life experience that people who were willing to look at their own personal histories are better able to make changes that produce a more satisfying life without regrets. The following concepts can recreate the promise of hopefulness the reader may have forgotten:

- Self-awareness

The reader can become aware of the attitudes that either limit or expand life.

- Conscious living

Conscious living implies choices based on today's reality; unconscious living is acting on lifelong patterns that have little bearing on the present.

- Awakening to wholeness

Many believe that a sense of being unfulfilled is a result of somehow being "broken." When people learn that this feeling, this condition of discomfort, is only a nudge to awaken, they can rediscover their own wholeness and regain a sense of hope that by the end of life, it will have been lived fully.

Wising Up creates a sense of hopefulness, reassures that life has meaning, and instructs how to find that meaning. The book provides methods to increase consciousness and broaden those narrowed perspectives. Through my own experience, as well as the teachings of others, you will learn the process involved in self-discovery and greater attentiveness to living.

Having been at the forefront of the Human Potential Movement of the 1960s and '70s, I am well-suited as a guide to aging boomers and others who want a more fulfilling life. My participation and leadership during this and succeeding periods allow me to provide tools to enlighten and motivate. Participate in *Wising Up* and live life without regrets.

Hal Milton

Napa, California

2004

ACKNOWLEDGEMENTS

Great appreciation is due to:

The many students, clients, workshop and class participants who became my teachers.

Those wonderful friends and my family who put up with my craziness as I attempted to put my ideas together.

My wife Sonya, who was at the beginning and end of my varied emotions, thoughts, and wonderings as I found ways and people to assist me. I appreciate her willingness to be patient as well as being a great sounding board and meticulous creative editor.

Marie Ross, who challenged many of my ideas, which ultimately helped clarify the points I was attempting to make, and then, as my editor, worked tirelessly at putting my thoughts on paper in a way that could be understood.

Rachel Harris, for her faith and assistance in the beginning. She helped me put my values and intentions into an outline form and, along the way, helped me with objectivity in the process of publishing.

Paul Block and Deborah Price, who provided organizational thoughts that assisted me in formulating the manuscript in a coherent manner.

Cate Merritt, my copy editor, who began and ended this process with me while providing encouragement, feedback, and clarification.

Kathy Mawer for her time and expertise for a final read.

Janna Waldinger, www.artclarity.com for the cover photograph.

Irina Rozo for her creative assistance in cover design and color.

DEDICATION

I dedicate this book to my life guides, who taught me the value of *process*: Claudio Naranjo, Ida Rolf, Bob Hoffman, Judith Aston, Laurence Mathae, and to my wife Sonya, who teaches me daily.

TABLE OF CONTENTS

The Choice to Live or Unlive Our Lives

I will not die an unlived life.
I will not live in fear of falling or catching fire.
I choose to inhabit my days.
to allow my living to open me.
to make me less afraid.
more accessible.
to loosen my heart
until it becomes a wing,
a torch, a promise.
I choose to risk my significance.
to live so that which came to me as seed
goes to the next as blossom.
and that which came to me as blossom,
goes on as fruit.

Dawna Markova

INTRODUCTION

Your journey in life is truly an adventure! As we grow older, something most of us need is a way of adding life to our years. The mere extension of years does not add value. Most of us want to leave an important legacy for those who will follow us. This legacy is actually the sharing of wisdom of our life experiences.

Wising Up is intended to integrate your relationships and all aspects of being human so that you may feel fulfilled, recognize your wholeness, and live a more conscious life.

How wonderful it would be if —as we move forward on our life journeys—we were to stop periodically to re-evaluate how we want to live. Are the choices we made (career? marriage? children? divorce?) as fulfilling as we had expected them to be? It takes courage and openness to explore our interior fabric at any age. Often we need to be told we are on the right track. It is challenging to be alone on the journey. We need support.

My hope is to provide you with a map or guide that will allow you to trust yourself (a process that occurs as you learn what "made you the way you are") and do that which enlivens and fulfills your life, so you may move into your elder years with grace and confidence.

When I realized I was getting older and my energy for "slaying dragons" was diminishing, I began looking toward retirement or at least semi-retirement. This view of my future was less comforting than I had imagined. *Who* I am had always been defined by *what* I did. Who was I—if I wasn't a coach, Rolfer® (a system of deep tissue manipulation focused on release of habitual stress-causing patterns), minister, or teacher? My whole life had been one directed toward achievement and reaching goals; now what would I be? What had worked for me in the past did not work as well as I became older. Feeling lost, I threw myself into activities that I thought I wanted to do, such as studying music. When my limited talent and aging mind made progression too slow to be fulfilling, I moved on. I began studying the aging process with the idea that I would create teachings to assist others with the aging process, using all the history and discoveries along my own path. These evolved into successful workshops, and they are what this book is about: adventures in aging – a journey we all share from the moment we're born.

This journey happens to be two-fold. True, we are born into a world of human beings, but we are also spiritual beings. Often, the rigors of being human cause us to lose our connection with our spiritual bases. This book addresses both of these aspects, both human and spiritual. The division of this book is somewhat overlapping, like life itself. Many ideas are expressed in various ways throughout the book because repetition is important in the learning process. Repetition with intention embodies the new ideas, so you can transform your life into conscious living rather than existing at the whim of your emotions and past conditioning. Each chapter ends with ideas to ponder and steps to take, assisting with challenges as you move into each new stage of maturation. The end result is a comprehensive toolbox: you will gain tools to deal with growing older, become more aware of your wholeness, and live more fully on your life journey.

By using the tools given you throughout this book, recalling your personal life story, allowing yourself to become involved in the *Things to do* sections at the end of each chapter, and keeping a journal, you are on the path to a fulfilling life and becoming a wise elder.

Before you even begin the first chapter, you can start "harvesting" your life experiences in a journal. I'll share with you how I did mine and offer suggestions so you can begin your own.

Every journey begins with the first step.

If you are asking yourself, "Why should I review my life? I don't see the need," this message, then, is for you. It has been said (in reference to all of us) that "You live a crooked life until you get your history straight!"

We are invited to be concerned with saving our life experiences by passing them on to others. For instance, I began doing my inner work in my early thirties. I have done (and continue to do) life reviews periodically. I peruse old photo albums and recall all the events from my past that those photos evoke, then I journal my feelings about them.

Keeping a journal, writing letters to loved ones, and expressing your inner thoughts are all ways to do this inner work. I regularly make a list of things I have done in my life – good and bad. Part of my process is to recall all the "folks who did me wrong." I use the idea from the 23rd Psalm, "Thou preparest a table before me in the presence of mine enemies." I have found many wonderful blessings from looking at what I thought had been "wrong."

A pearl forms from sand irritation. So I have looked also to those folks whom I felt had hurt me and determined how that hurt worked for me in my life. I also look at what failures motivated me to success. Looking at my most painful experiences that have been tucked away for ages has been golden for me. I found that these painful times have led to many of my greatest successes.

Many of us want to forget our painful and uncomfortable experiences, erase the images from our memories the same way we can erase files from our computers. Yet, these very memories can serve us —can free us — when we see that they've been influencing us all along without our conscious knowledge. Those of us who have worked on our computers and forgotten to save a file, only to have it lost forever when the computer crashed, face the same fate should our human memories fail. We should be equally concerned about what is going to happen to our life experiences if we don't save them for review.

The process of remembering is more important than the end result; this is a difficult concept to ingest since we each have much conditioning to achieve a goal rather than to focus on the journey. The result is like magic, and transformation can happen. The gold is in the process!

I interpret a passage from the Gospel of Thomas to say:

> If you bring forth what is inside you, what you bring forth will save you.
>
> If you do not bring forth what is inside you, what you do not bring forth will destroy you.
>
> Thomas: 3.

For each of us to tell our own story is not only important, it's therapeutic. This harvest is one way to help us "know ourselves." Chronicle each year of your life.

Every circumstance, every situation, every event was and is an opportunity to grow closer to Spirit and to "know thyself." At the end of a long life, the Hasidic Rabbi Zusia said, "In the world to come no one will ask me why was I not Moses. I shall be asked, 'Why were you not Zusia?'"

Looking back at our life experiences is a big step toward discovering our soul and our life patterns; it can bring us to a point of action. Remember, this harvesting process is ongoing. Our final step is not lying back, but involvement and concern for our fellow travelers. I have heard it said, "We repair the past and prepare for the future by living in the present." Our choice is the way we choose to view the experiences in life as well as self-examination. That is how wisdom is gained. Once our inner work has begun – and it really is continuous—then we can find ways to share our wisdom. We can join a service group, find a person to mentor, or perform a public service; let's be creative. The opportunity for service may simply appear.

Collect the Pieces

The gold of your intelligence
is scattered over many clippings and bits
of wanting. Bring them all together
in one place. How else can I stamp it?
Think how great a city concentrates
around a point. Damascus or Samarcand.
Grain by grain, collect the pieces.
The Beloved then becomes food and water,
lamp and helper, dessert and wine.
Many-ness is confusion and intellectual talk.
Silence gives answers. I know that,
but my mouth keeps opening involuntarily
Like a yawn or a sneeze.

Rumi (Barks 121)

At the conclusion of each chapter in *Wising Up,* you will find a section called "*What you can do.*" These exercises have been specially designed for you to more fully embody the material presented. These *"things to do"* can be done as you complete the chapter, or you can refer back to them as your time and interest permit.

CHAPTER 1

THE ADVENTURE OF AGING

Ever since I can remember I have been exploring a variation of the question, "What do I want to do when I grow up?" My own journey has mutated the question to, "What do I want to do now that I am grown up?"

Some time ago I taught a class entitled "Six Months to Live," at Unity Church in Napa Valley (California) and found that merely looking at death in a conscious way brought up anxieties for many. Much of this anxiety seems to be about getting older and losing the attributes of youth. Loose or flabby skin and facial lines replace the taut, firm look of youth. Agility and physical strength diminish. Women have the dubious enjoyment of hot flashes, while men spend longer time at the urinal.

For both sexes, memory becomes less reliable, and there is a tendency to shake one's head and simply acknowledge that one is having another of those senior moments. Sexuality changes for both sexes – usually with diminished sex drive. The urgency that drove one in youth seems to have suddenly acquired patience. Men have sometimes simply lost the ability, although with Viagra that may be changing.

And finally, we are concerned about PURPOSE — a big one for me and, I am certain, for others too. "Who am I now that I am no longer as productive economically?"

Once when I was at the gym about to enter the locker room, a teenager stepped aside and opened the door for me. At first I was shocked because I didn't see myself as old, but I soon realized that he did. Then I discovered how good it felt to be respected in that way. As I have learned to accept my aging and not wish for the return of youth, I feel much happier.

Most folks don't want to accept the aging process — little wonder with our culture's attitude honoring youth. Even the magazines that cater to the aged usually show advertisements with youthful-appearing adults to sell their products. In many other cultures age is revered. These cultures have wisdom circles and sages, passing the knowledge and wisdom gained from life experiences to the succeeding generations.

Attitudes on Life and Death

From *Fifty-two* by Michael Vextua comes this wisdom:

> When adults of other eras taught their young to "respect your elders," they were respecting the Old One who lived within each young person—strengthening the Old One, giving the Old One a source of pride, so that it would be up to the task when it was needed. But our culture insults and shames the Old One at every turn, so we are left with only the Young One with which to face infirmity and death. But the Young One is unprepared for this, for the Young One is incapable of believing in death. With its audacity, the Young One gives us great strength, at the proper time. But that time passes. And after it passes, only the Old One can give us the strength we need.

Without wisdom circles and sages advising us of what to expect while we are "adding years to our lives," we focus primarily on the deterioration of our physical bodies. We begin to look and feel different from our younger selves: skin becomes looser, our vision loses acuity, our weight and metabolism change, and those senior moments of forgetfulness frustrate us.

Sometime in my mid-fifties I noticed that I was beginning to lose strength and my coordination was altered. I wasn't as agile; my body responded more slowly than it had. That was difficult for an old "jock" — difficult, because my "Young One" could only keep me focused on what I had lost, rather than what I had gained. My discomfort with this focus compelled me to find and nurture my "Old One" – the one who provided me a different kind of strength and a new attitude.

Speaking of attitudes, there is a book that I read several years ago – a wonderful book called *Mists of Avalon* by Marion Zimmer Bradley. It is a mythical allusion to the tales of King Arthur. Avalon is a magical island that is hidden behind huge impenetrable mists. Unless the mists part, there is no way to navigate to the island. But unless you *believe* the island is there, the mists won't part.

Avalon symbolizes a world beyond the world we see with our physical eyes. It is the truth of who we really are and that truth doesn't go away just because the mists hide it. I relate Avalon to TRUTH, SPIRIT, and LOVE. These don't go away because we don't perceive or use them. The truth of their existence merely gets clouded over or surrounded by mental mists. However, these truths are easily retrieved because *perception, or belief, is a choice,* and the choice is always ours.

The mists part when we believe that Avalon is beyond them. Instead of the attitude, "I'll believe it when I see it," try the attitude, "I'll *see* it when I *believe* it." That is what our transformation is all about—a parting of the mists, a shift in perception.

Attitudes are developed over time. What we believe becomes the framework of how we live our lives. This may not be a shattering awareness, but in order to understand our attitudes toward aging or toward any experience, we need to examine where our beliefs arise in our lives. Sometimes this can be quite uncomfortable; however, if we want to get a handle on our behavior, we need to be willing to explore our inner processes and histories. As we begin to comprehend the fabric of our make-up, we can then have an opportunity to change. In many cases, mere awareness can create change without any further understanding on our part. It seems that the process of exploration does the work.

In late childhood and early teens, we generally can't wait to get older. The continual barrage of rhetoric from those who care for us say something like this: "Wait till you grow up;" "You'll have plenty of time to do that;" or "You're too young—you don't understand." Add your own admonition that was given you. The message was that you're too young to know. We can hardly wait to age, so we will "know" and can do the things we want without interference. In many instances the message is true, yet that message is not very helpful when we are just beginning to develop self-confidence and appropriate attitudes.

The following is another perspective on aging. Helen M. Luke takes it from Kaleidoscope "*The Way of Woman*" *and Other Essays.*

> I received notice of a seminar to be given by Adolf Guggenbuhl-Craig in New York on "Aging." In the summary of his theme it is said that he suggests it is time to see aging as a process of becoming free . . . "the real archetypal image, the stimulating symbol for the aging would be, not the wise old man or woman, but the 'foolish' old man or woman," then they would find freedom from all conventions and will not care if they show their deficiencies. They would be able to let go of all need to be wise and to do the right thing; they could admit now that they don't understand the world anymore. The archetype would be more accurately described as the Fool and the Child within us rather than as "foolish." The freedom of the Fool and the Child is never silly; it is Sophia "playing in the world."

As we age and begin participating in the adult world, all the input we get is to stay young. Youth is valued in our culture, so we begin to think there is something wrong with aging. We attempt to stay the aging process. Our attitude dreads getting old. I am not saying we shouldn't do things to keep our health and vitality, but resistance to the aging process can cause much discomfort, particularly as we begin to lose some of our physical acuteness; i.e. failing vision, diminished coordination, and aches and pains from imbalances in the body. Getting older can be a rich and meaningful process of our lives. We can develop a positive attitude about aging and be proud of the symptoms of aging; we can live more fully in our maturing years. We may choose how we perceive any situation during our aging process. Therefore, since we have the choice, why not look at the unavoidable in a positive way that uplifts us rather than brings us down?

" . . . there is nothing either good or bad, but thinking makes it so."

Hamlet — by William Shakespeare

As I counsel and work with elders of all ages, the common fear is that they haven't lived. Their dreams haven't been fulfilled. Society is just beginning to pay attention to elders. There aren't a whole lot of models for the delights of being an elder. When we view magazines focusing on the aged, we see advertisements with golf trips and cruises—things we couldn't afford when we were younger. The focus is on entertainment and distraction. How about enjoying and feeling fulfilled from our life experiences? Many of us don't take the time to gather those experiences of life and bring them to conscious awareness. When we take the time to do this, however, we can learn how much we have achieved and take pride. We can then move ahead with confidence as we have fun.

In my workshops "Preparing to Become An Elder," I use a system of gathering life experiences that has come from my study with Dr. Claudio Naranjo, Bob Hoffman of the Hoffman Quadrinity Process of psycho-spiritual integration, and Rabbi Zalman Schachter-Shalomi, who has devoted part of his elder years to raising the consciousness of the benefits of aging in his book, *From Age-ing to Sage-ing*, with Ronald S. Miller.

"This above all: To thine own self be true,

And it must follow, as the night the day,

Thou canst not then be false to any man."

Hamlet — by William Shakespeare

To *know ourselves* is age-old advice that I feel is particularly valuable as we evaluate our next step in the process of getting older. Wisdom comes from knowledge and experience.

Rabbi Schacter-Shalomi's theory is that by the time we have reached middle age we begin to spend more time searching our inner selves to discover the meaning of life. However, most folks avoid doing this work. If our elder years are to have more meaning than golf, vacations, and puttering around the house, this inner work can't be avoided.

Sometimes, though, we need to put some energy into changing behavior or attitudes if they are deeply conditioned into our personalities.

In my earlier book, *Going Public: A Practical Guide to Developing Personal Charisma*, I explain how we are born stars, perfect children of and perfect expressions of God. That *Star,* that *Child,* may also be called Soul, Spirit, the Christ Within, or Buddha-nature. Whatever you call it, the *Star* is that part of each of us that is in union with the Divine. As we grow and mature, we develop layers of conditioning that encapsulate the *Star* and build layers between our connections to the Divine.

We are taught how to live in our culture: "Don't touch yourself that way;" "Don't go near the street or in that yard;" and "Don't open the door when I'm not here." Much of what we are told is for our safety. But many of us interpret these reprimands as meaning there is something wrong with us, not just with our behavior. We begin to identify with many of the negatives that come our way and lose the awareness of our Star. We begin to believe that we are the "bad boy" or "naughty girl" — the bundle of mistakes that adults keep pointing out.

"I often hate in self defense.

If I were more enlightened, I would not have used such a tool."

— Kahlil Gibran

As children, we often can't differentiate between *making* a mistake and *being* a mistake. This is when we develop a layer of self-concept that contains all the "bad" parts of ourselves. Since we don't want anyone to see this "bad part," we begin to learn behaviors to hide that first layer. Then we develop a second layer: our armor. This layer consists of various certifications, qualifications and labels that we use to puff up our fragile sense of self. "See how great I am. I'm a doctor, teacher, platinum-card carrier, you-name-it." We use these "validations" to prove to the world that we are all right.

When someone gets close enough to see Layer One, we become quite defensive. We really only wanted Layer Two to be seen. Layer One makes us feel "less than" our carefully refined image in Layer Two. The truth is that although both layers may be necessary to help us get along in the world, they may also become obstacles to the expression of our Star, our spiritual being.

Spirit: we all have it, but what is it? One definition is that Spirit is God in each and every one of us. In fact, the word Spirit is interchangeable with the word God, and God is known by many names: *Spirit, Higher Self/Higher Power, Buddha, Buddha-nature, Christ, Allah, Great Spirit*; and, of course, the beliefs that assign a god's name to a specific Power, as the Hindus and the ancient Greeks and Romans had done. Spirit can be felt or sensed in that we can feel a spiritual connection with others. We can feel Spirit when we "let go" and open our hearts and minds. An intuition, or hunch, is Spirit-sent. Spirit includes rather than separates. Spirit doesn't judge; it accepts.

Some folks confuse religion with spirituality, but the two are different. Underlying Religion is Spirit. Where Religion is philosophical and dogmatic, Spirit has no philosophy, no dogma. Religion can sometimes divide, but Spirit always unites. Spirit is awareness, the deep knowing that surpasses intellectual understanding. Spirit is the great "Ah-hah."

Throughout the rest of this book, the word *Spirit* will be substituted or interchanged with the word *God.* Any term for *God* or *Spirit* is just as acceptable. And now it is time for you to become active in this process of getting to know yourself.

What you can do:

First thing to do

A major part of these "things to do" involves writing. I suggest using a loose-leaf binder as your journal, so you can add pages throughout this process. I find that writing seems to assist in crystallizing memories in a way that just thinking doesn't do. However, I realize that some people are more comfortable speaking than writing. If so, I urge you to speak your memories into a tape recorder. If you choose to use this method, your oral history will need to be transcribed in order to carry out the succeeding steps. Our thoughts are ephemeral and quickly transition from one topic to another. Getting a handle on our true beliefs requires us to make them more concrete – by putting our thoughts on paper.

Begin by journaling some of your beliefs and attitudes about aging. In what ways are you resistant to or accepting of this process of aging?

Second thing to do

Search your memory of your experiences from the womb to the present. USE A SEPARATE PAGE FOR EACH YEAR (except for the first five years, which can be condensed on one page). You can call this section your Chronological Journal. Recall statements heard, attitudes perceived, how you were disciplined or taught. Don't worry if those early times are merely imaginative; write them anyway. They come from your mind. Focus on each age and write your recollections. Notice which of those that you feel are positive and those you perceive as negative.

Third thing to do

At each chronological age recollect significant moments or events that impacted you: a hospital stay, surgery, an accident, a memorable vacation, or an embarrassing moment.

Fourth thing to do

Who were the persons or person that guided or influenced you along the way, either positively or negatively? Who hurt you? Notice what is attached to each parent or surrogate caregiver (e.g. "Mother always scolded; Father always hit." Or, "Mom always loved and Dad was always angry." Or "Mother seemed fearful; Father was supportive.")

Fifth thing to do

What or how did each age or age group influence who you are today? Journal.

Sixth thing to do

Whom did you hurt? Take your time with this. Add to it as you remember. Working in one age may stimulate a memory of an event or person in another age. Go back and add to it. (This is why the loose-leaf binder is effective: you can add pages.) This study is an ongoing process – no benefit is gained by rushing through it.

CHAPTER 2

WAKING UP: BECOMING FULLY CONSCIOUS

In the Bible, 1 Kings 19:11-12, Elijah is told to "stand upon the mount before the Lord. And behold, the Lord passed by, and a great and strong wind rent the mountains, and broke in pieces the rocks before the Lord, but the Lord was not in the wind; and after the wind an earthquake, but the Lord was not in the earthquake; and after the earthquake a fire; but the Lord was not in the fire; and after the fire a still, small voice."

We seem to expect Spirit to come in the most dramatic forms – the "burning bush" if you will — yet it is the "still small voice" we need to heed. And how do we hear that still, small voice? How do we learn to hear it? We learn to listen. "Be still and know that I am God." (Psalms 46:10)

The middle years are upon us – and with them, the sensation (the Call or Awakening) that something is missing that we can't quite put our fingers on. All on the outside seems to be going well, but there is a divine discomfort within. The little inner voice keeps nagging. Life was supposed to be different, somehow. We may have good work, a family, a home and all the things for which we have been striving all these years. We feel that the pleasures have not been equal to the energy and time we've paid into our "life accounts." Where is the return on our investment? We have come a long way, but what is in store for the rest of our lives? Where will we find the joy and the fulfillment? Is it really possible? And we are getting older. Is this all there is? There is purpose in our merely asking these questions.

When we are young, we are usually so ego-driven that we think we are in charge of our destinies. To some extent, that is true. But now our destinies are not measuring up to our dreams – how can we live as fully as possible? How can we get to enjoy those things we always thought would give us joy? Some of us may have love affairs or impulsively buy something new – a car, a house, a new article of clothing. We work harder, or we think about travel. Not that any of these things are wrong – the more important thing is to know what is driving us. What is the dissatisfaction? One question kept popping up in my thinking: If these are my best years, why do I feel so empty?

Let's look at the process of aging. What happens? How does it work? How can our brains and bodies change so much during a lifetime, yet in our minds we still feel young or somehow ageless? We still think of ourselves as youthful. We may admit, "I'm getting older," but the reality, at least for me, is that I feel vibrant and will live to a very old age. I doubt that I am alone in this thinking.

Our own aging comes to us as somewhat of a surprise. We seem to fairly readily accept the physical and mental aging process – in others! I remember my father, when he was way up in his eighties, telling me what he would do in his old age – that is to say, when he got there. He did not seem to have a clue that his train had already pulled into that station.

Books are full of information dividing our lives into sections, for example: infancy, childhood, youth, early adult life, mid-life transitions, middle adult years, and elderly. We tend to accept these sectional divisions of our lives because similar thoughts and emotions arise with all people during distinct stages, even though the ages of these stages may vary from person to person. We understand that, as humans, we continue to evolve throughout the course of our lives and that each stage brings with it experiences that are important for growth leading to the next stage. What we do with the experience is more important to our well-being, self-confidence, and maturation than the experience itself.

An important aspect of our evolution is spirituality – an aspect that in our general culture seems to be somehow overlooked or given halfhearted attention. Although lip service is paid to the virtue of having spirituality, not much care is lavished on the importance of how and what we think in this regard. Perhaps this is ONE of the elements missing that keeps us from feeling full. Not the only one, but one that could be easily overlooked. So, what is the spiritual element? What does that mean?

Physical and mental aging are easier passages for us to accept because they are fairly apparent. Our spiritual journeys, however, are not so easily viewed, not concrete at all. Spiritual passages, though, are as real as the social and psychological ones that are well documented. They simply require more awareness from us to note the transitions.

Viewing the structure of the many great religions and spiritual teachings of the world – Christianity, Judaism, Buddhism, Islam, Hinduism, Taoism etc. – I see that all are rooted in the idea of progressive developmental passages.

Where we start:

We can begin at any time we are ready to investigate ourselves. The process is simple, but perhaps not easy. One has to be sincere in looking at each motivation of behavior to witness where that idea came from. Did I choose this idea or belief, or was it given to me by a parent, a caregiver, society or my peer group? What causes me to believe or feel the way I do? How do I respond to that which comes into my life?

The Gospel writers tell us, along with every spiritual teaching I know, to awaken; we are asleep. "Arise," the New Testament tells us over and over again, and "awake." What are we to arise or awake from? Perhaps it is from our rote behavior, our operating as if on "auto-pilot." Perhaps we need to awaken that which is already present within us, to begin exploring our inner journeys so that we may "know" ourselves.

A call to awaken can come in many forms: an intuition, a chance meeting, an idea from a book – and <u>ONE</u> of the forms is the FALL. A fall would be something that seems to have gone wrong: you lost your job, your spouse asked for a divorce, your child got into trouble at school. In other words, something dramatic happens in life that disrupts our well-being. This disruption occurs for a reason: it is designed to AWAKEN us, so we may learn a lesson that will promote the soul's growth.

The more conscious and open to Spirit we are as these lessons unfold, the easier our journey becomes.

We don't often look at a FALL as a CALL or awakening.

Earlier in the book, I mentioned the incident with the teenager at the gym who opened the door for me, prompting my sudden realization that others saw me as an older man. I had been awakened to that truth.

One of my daughters had a recent experience that "awakened" her. One of her emotional "buttons" was pushed, causing her to dramatically alter her life path. When we talked, she said she realized that this incident was one of a long line of these kinds of reactions.

This was an experience that finally got her to look at her pattern. It was a wake-up call that got her to listen. She deduced that her impulsive reactions had been attempts to show what she had thought of as a masculine power that her "female" wasn't going to be "run over."

Sometimes we need to be defeated again and again (our so-called "fall") before the "light" brings us illumination and understanding—just as my daughter needed one defeat after another until her final defeat brought the great "ah-hah!"

Thus, our lives happen in *Divine Order.* Events enter our lives and teach us the lessons needed to build our wisdom. The more open we are to ACCEPTING these events with an attitude of gratitude, the easier they are for us to handle. This takes practice. The practice isn't easy, but it's worth training our thinking to make it so.

Perhaps Meister Eckhart says it best as to where we begin, "The eye with which I see God is the eye with which God sees me." God is not a man with a long white beard up in the sky. God is in me—we are ONE. This notion is a great beginning.

The process of discovering is more important than the result. This process is the gold, the wine, the juice that can enliven us, so we don't come to the end of our lives feeling as if we have never lived.

Our preoccupation with worldly matters keeps us in the dark – unawakened, asleep. How can I stop to breathe and enjoy all that I have worked so hard and long to attain?

There are experiences or events that come into existence to help us along the path of evolution. These are put in our paths to help awaken us to the knowledge that there is more. The "more" is the inner search of discovering the "who I am." What is the relationship between our inner and outer lives?

For many years I felt lost. I did not know who I was anymore. I was going along, doing what was in front of me, and completely doing those tasks I thought I was *supposed* to do and be for my stage of life. But the truth was that I was merely filling time by "doing," so I would not feel the discomfort of not knowing. Our culture encourages us to become human "doings" rather than human "beings." Rarely will you find

"Spirit" in the arena of business. The focus is on production or "the bottom line."

I am reminded of a story told by the Sufi poet, Rumi: There was a reed taken from its reed bed in a lake and made into a flute; and to this day whenever the flute is played, the song tells of its yearning for the home it was separated from. We have all been taken from a reed bed, and our discontent will probably continue as long as we feel that sense of separation.

In truth, we are never separated, but we have the *sense* of separation; what is really important is to simply realize this truth and begin to start searching so we can embody it. The search itself will be an instrument to help us evolve. It is necessary for us to get to a point in our process where we make the distinction as to what is important in life and then begin or continue our search.

Carl Jung, in his *Stages of Life* essay, expresses that "a person gropes toward wisdom, and a search for enduring personal values begins. Either we begin a quest for meaning at mid-life, or we become simply an applauder of the past, an eternal adolescent—all lamentable substitutes for the illumination of the self." He goes on to say that by our *not* beginning the inner search at some time does damage to the soul.

The search for life's purpose can begin at any age, but it is helpful if a person has lived long enough and made enough mistakes to recognize that an unexamined life goes nowhere.

We begin by recognizing that we want more. We feel driven to seek, and this is commonly known as *the divine discomfort*. This awareness sparks a search; it is an attempt to remember what we already know, but have temporarily forgotten.

We begin a quest for a spiritual exercise or practice that seems right for us.

Once we find some guidance (through a church, a temple or synagogue, a book, a spiritual practice, an enlightened mentor, or even a twelve-step program), we endure trials of discovery. We meet up with the dragons and devils of myths; however, now they are in our history, and we realize the patterns we have been living with. We have problems of depression, regret, impatience, futility and cynicism. Our habits are brought to consciousness. We must meet these head on—it is the turmoil of awakening. It is this very struggle that helps us along the path to enlightenment.

We become aware of who and what we are really made of. We discover those parts of ourselves that are connected. We begin to recognize that we are ONE with Spirit and there is something that changes within us that cannot be explained – only experienced. The experience of this knowing usually happens after or during the inner reflections.

We can become awakened at any age and in many different ways. We hear the still, small voice that tells us to do something else. It can be in a dream, during an illness, an experience, a struggle, a word. Just about anything can awaken us to something different. It is our job to keep listening to what is happening in our lives. Many times we pay no attention to the voice because we are not attuned to listening to something so small and still. But when we finally decide to listen, to truly heed the message, our movement is always toward spirit even though it may not seem that way. I might add that we are not who we think we are. There is more to us than meets the eye – even our own eye. I think we view ourselves from our five senses – touch, smell, taste, sight, hearing – but there is more. From my days of Rolfing I learned that our bodies store memories like onions: they need to be peeled off in layers. There are deep layers of the mind that need to be peeled back in the same way so the beauty of "the deep" can rise to the surface.

The soul or spirit communicates with our depth in many ways: through dreams, sacred art, paintings, music, chants, sacred books, suffering, and through spiritual practice, i.e. meditation, breath, dance, vision quests, and invocations. All of these methods are designed to suspend discursive thoughts and put us in direct contact with Spirit.

Although our bodies (our outsides) are adult, inside all of us there is the small child who may want an ice cream. We are continually in a push-pull relationship with our deep soul versus our everyday conscious with its own wants and desires. We are definitely a combination of the deep self and the self that has been shaped by environment. But we are the ones who made those choices all along the way. Generally, we think we are independent thinkers, but the reality is that we absorb patterns of behavior that are acceptable in our crowd. We are imitators.

It is so important to delve into our subconscious—to shine the light on that which is dark—in order to touch our spirit in a conscious way.

According to many spiritual traditions, our task is to rediscover the identity at our center. The bible tells us to become as little children – to become childlike, to uncover the tarnishing of layers of ego to reach into our center and touch the reality of spirit.

The middle years are just the right time for in-depth spiritual seeking. We need a certain amount of life experience to appreciate the need for understanding the deeper parts of ourselves. In old age we may not feel we have enough time nor the energy or motivation to complete the search. A few spiritual teachers will not accept a student until she or he is 35 or 40 years old. It seems that life experiences reflected by chronological age allow a person to ripen enough to be willing to explore inner space.

Philosopher Soren Kierkegaard once remarked, "We live life forward but only understand it backward." So we are invited to examine our lives in order to understand them.

Spiritual awakening is a process of unfoldment. It is not an event that happens all at once. When we were young we may have thought to take a designer drug or meditate, so we would have instant enlightenment. And happen it might, but most of us need to do the ego-reducing work, to get below the surface and experience what is present in a conscious way, so we will feel the joy of spirit. Ripening of age and experience seems to be necessary.

Psychologists tell us that during early adulthood – when we are in our twenties and early thirties – the ego is dominant. Our time is spent establishing our adult identities and getting ahead in a world that had previously belonged to our parents. Desire for spiritual growth is usually on hold, if indeed we are even aware of spirituality. During our thirties the desire for success intensifies and we adjust our self-images. We strengthen our mastery over the outer. Underneath, however, a faint voice still cries for us to come in. During our late thirties and early forties, we are usually at the height of our accomplishments and are usually seasoned citizens in our communities. Many of us, however, remain unfulfilled at a deeper level. The sense of accomplishment from the outer achievements doesn't last, and the real joy lies waiting in the heart and spirit.

These urgings to awaken might take the form of a chance meeting, a book, an event, perhaps a dream. Dreams carry valuable information for us. A Gnostic proverb makes this declaration: "A dream not considered is like a letter from God unopened." Dreams can be powerful spiritual messages.

First comes *awareness* – awakening from inertia to become motivated to take action and do something. Sitting still, if done with the right attitude, is doing something. What is the *right* attitude? Perhaps backing into this answer might provide more enlightenment. All of us have experienced arriving somewhere on time only to find we have to wait – for someone else to arrive, for something to begin. Usually this unanticipated outcome is accompanied by aggravation, anxiety, or just plain discomfort. We don't *want* to wait. Then we decide we will need to provide ourselves with some distraction to dispel the discomfort and make the waiting more bearable. In other words, any distraction will do as long as we are not just *sitting still.* So, what if we were to change this attitude of needing a distraction? Suppose we allowed ourselves to *just sit,* and in that *sitting with ourselves,* we simply practiced awareness: of ourselves in that situation, of the world around us, of our thoughts, of our feelings. And then, while we were practicing this awareness, suppose we then practiced *acceptance* – simply accepting all of which we were now aware, including negative thoughts and emotions. Because when we have *awareness* and *acceptance,* we don't have to act on our feelings. We can view all these things about and around ourselves from a slight distance, as though we're aware that we're watching a movie and are not the characters in that movie. From this perspective we can more calmly recognize choices that we can make. This, then, would be "sitting with the right attitude." If we continue to allow ourselves to "sit with the right attitude," we begin to notice that we have more connection with our insides, our intuition. The "still, small voice" is more clearly heard when we practice just sitting with ourselves. From this position, we are invited to bring forth what is inside us and live from the inside out.

So, our awareness brings us to the point of action, provided we choose to accept. Mid-life can be a time of "being" rather than "becoming," but how many of us do that? We continue to focus on "becoming" because we still feel so unfulfilled. When we "become" whatever it is we believe we need to become, we will finally be fulfilled, we think.

In the Gospels Jesus tells us that if we seek, we shall find. *Where do we seek?*

The first step is to trust that the seeking will reveal answers. We may have to pretend to believe, at first.

The second step is to look with our non-logical minds. Just be open to seeing. Many folks think nothing is happening because we are trained to look for something concrete. A word game offers a familiar word jumbled into something unrecognizable. "COBUNE" makes no sense and we may struggle in frustration to figure out its meaning. When we let go of the struggle, the word trying to be revealed, BOUNCE, makes its appearance.

The truth is that this is a big thing to become aware of. Boredom or depression is really a great light bulb shining brightly just so that we may see the old ways are not working anymore. Change has to happen if we are to continue progressing. We have grown out of the old ways. It's time to move on. If there is pain, then it may be that happiness is going through the pain, not running from it.

My belief is that every circumstance, every situation is an opportunity to grow closer to God. All events – even illness – enter our lives to help us on our journey back to our realization of our ONENESS with God. Pain or discomfort may be the bell to awaken us to the solution just waiting to be discovered. And we can invite this pain to run its course. I think the attitude we bring toward each event or circumstance in life holds the key to happiness. If we look at all events as gifts and search for the "yes" in them rather than the "no"—life becomes smoother. With less resistance, with less fear, with trust in the "yes," the rocks on our paths turn to sand, the cresting waves turn to gentle swells, and we make our way in life with more ease of well-being.

Do we create our own illusions? Why can't I just "be?" Many of us ask these questions after working hard much of life into our fifties and sixties. Yet we keep going—feeling we need to keep producing or . . . . Or what? We rarely even ask that question, so we never get around to answering it. We make up this need for being productive in our own minds. We can usually do whatever we want once we decide it's what we want. The decision gets mixed up with what others think is best for us and our own thoughts and feelings. In my life, I have come to a place in my early seventies that doesn't require me to slay dragons, yet I keep going, keep producing. I ask myself, why? The answer comes that I have consciously chosen to be active, that I WANT to. However, I also consciously choose my activities rather than "having" to do them. I <u>always</u> had my choice, I now realize, but I am aware of it.

What you can do:

First thing to do

Where in life was a Fall or Call? Journal your recollections.

Second thing to do

Add to your "Chronological Journal" those unresolved conflicts or regrets, grief, guilt, and unfulfilled dreams, as well as becoming conscious of those people and events that were positive in your life. This is the brunt of much spiritual work. "Know yourself." It is one of the greatest spiritual tasks any of us may undertake. Consequently, it is vital.

Third thing to do

Consider attending a church, support group, or spiritual community if you don't already attend one of these. If you already have one of the above, then consider exploring a different one, even if you attend a church with a different faith or attend a 12-step group – something with a different focus than your present one. (Check your local hospitals, HMOs, newspapers, meditation groups, etc. for support groups or teachings.) By challenging yourself in this way you may discover how the experience "feeds" you.

In every teaching there is something to be gained. There are many paths; explore how other paths arrive at the same Truth.

CHAPTER 3

THE WISDOM IN PAYING ATTENTION

This is a story about Abraham, as told in Genesis. The story goes that Abraham was living in an astonishingly beautiful location with his wife Sarah. They were comfortable, quite happy, and very rich with many possessions: cattle, silver, and gold, and we're told he may have had a vineyard.

Then it happened. One day Abraham received a message:

> Now the Lord said to Abraham, 'Go from your country and your kindred and your father's house to the land that I will show you. And I will make of you a great nation, and I will bless you, and make your name great, so that you will be a blessing. I will bless those who bless you, and him who curses you I will curse;

and by you all the families of the earth will bless themselves.'

Genesis 12:1-3.

What do you suppose you would you do if you received such a clear message? Would you be paying enough attention to recognize it was a message from Spirit? Well, Abraham did, and, of course, went! He left his comfort, took his wife and all his wealth, and hit the road.

In our more modern world, I think of the many ways people are uprooted or just pick up and leave. Folks left their comfort on the east coast, paid attention, heard a call, and settled the west. Immigrants left Europe and came to America. During wars people have had to leave their homes – some, never to return. Floods, earthquakes, fires, storms – all have forced people to leave.

Spirit speaks to us in lots of ways. We don't normally view natural calamities as a voice from Spirit, but think about it! Nothing happens – good or bad, as we choose to view it.

Within each of our personal stories there is an invitation to PAY ATTENTION! Spirit invites us to probe for a rich opportunity to discover a little more about ourselves.

What is behind or hiding under our story?

Might it have been the voice of Spirit in one of its many forms?

I remember talking to several of my friends in the Los Angeles area after one of their big earthquakes, and their communication to me was very clear: "We're out of here." In their cases, the calamity was the voice heard.

In my own life, my wife Sonya and I were living in East Tennessee. We were ministers at an established Unity church. We lived close to a health club, which was important to us. We enjoyed the varied seasons of that part of the country; we had a delightful large home, as we were able to buy a home very reasonably in that area. It all seemed quite wonderful. Yet, there was a divine unrest in me. I was not happy. I could not understand this unrest because everything was nearly perfect.

I began to probe the unrest, and I realized that I had been visited with this unrest many times in my life. There was always a "something" that urged me on. More importantly, in the midst of the unrest there seemed to be an inner struggle in making a decision of some kind.

As I reflect on my days in high school, when I was agonizing over the decision to attend college, I was told not to go by a high school teacher – that I would never make it. But the urge became strong, and although fearful, I did it anyway and earned an advanced degree. I was then hired to teach physical education and science at the local junior high school, but my dream was to coach football at the high school.

So when the opportunity came to be part of the football coaching staff at the high school, I was quite excited but scared as well. Scared because I now had three children and coaching was a tentative position. My wife (at that time) encouraged me to stay where I was. There was too much uncertainty with coaching, and we needed the security of staying in the area.

Once again I agonized with the decision, but the inner urge was too strong, so I accepted the position. The following year, the head coach left, and I was selected to replace him. (I had been PAYING ATTENTION and became willing to ACT on those inner urges.)

I found that raising three children on a teacher's salary became a rigorous challenge, so I began to focus on how to make more money. A real estate broker friend told me I could become licensed, make extra money, and he would sponsor me. Once more I debated inwardly but finally decided this was an opportunity.

I studied for the real estate test and eventually became licensed, left teaching and coaching, and began a successful real estate brokerage firm. One day a colleague told me about a meditation that was proving to be quite helpful for him. Something inside me said YES, so I took instruction from a local teacher, began meditating, and my life has never been the same.

I was led to a variety of therapeutic and spiritual experiences, which in turn led me to change professions again. Still paying attention, I was directed to a wise old woman, Dr. Ida P. Rolf, who invited me into her training program. Soon I became a Rolf®[1] practitioner. (For those unfamiliar with Rolfing, it is a system of body therapy which aligns and integrates body, mind, emotion, and spirit.)

Eventually, Sonya and I met (I was long-divorced from my first wife by this time)—she was a Rolfer, too. We entered into a relationship, and both of us had full Rolfing practices in beautiful Santa Barbara, where we lived in a nourishing environment with a home on a hill with views of both the ocean and mountains.

In the midst of all this serenity, my divine unrest poked at me again, but this time I had a partner with whom to share decision-making. My wife and I were members of a Unity Church and were aligned with the teachings that told us the powers were within us rather than outside us. The mystical aspects of honoring our own experience "spoke" to us more eloquently than the dogma of other religions, so, with some anxiety, we left our comfort behind in the mountains of Santa Barbara to enter Unity School of Religious Studies (now named

[1] Rolfing is a service mark of the Rolf Institute of Structural Integration.

Unity Institute), in Missouri with the plan to become ordained Unity ministers.

Each time I made a move, I experienced fear and anxiety. I struggled with new decisions, but every move took me to new levels of my spiritual development. Each event was Spirit nudging me to mindfulness. It is only in retrospect that I see that I was guided all along the way. It was my responsibility to PAY ATTENTION, to TRUST, and to ACT.

I still suffer in making some decisions, even the most trivial. I recall a time when my outdoor garage light went out. Now I realize that I have many talents but handyman is not one of them. "Some assembly required" is a major undertaking for me. So even though my talents aren't in the area of repairing, I felt compelled to attempt to repair the garage light. After all, I am a man, and men are supposed to know these things. It was suggested I get a new fixture because it wasn't worth my time to attempt to fix it. I struggled with that since one of my neuroses is that nothing must go to waste. I thought about replacing the socket or repairing the wiring or something. The fixture seemed perfectly good to me. Waste not; want not, you know.

Anyway, I succumbed and finally bought a new fixture and had a friend help me put it up. It looks much better than the old one, and I was able to get a fluorescent bulb, thereby making it more energy efficient. Still, I had had to struggle with that decision for a week. It's actually easier for me to pick up and move across the country than to make a decision about a light fixture.

After all that decision-making, I wound up ordering another fixture for the porch. Lately, my spiritual work is to NOT make those kinds of things so important. They are not worth my energy. I have more important things on which to focus.

It's funny, when I'm asked to do this or that workshop or give this or that presentation—I usually say yes and then figure the "how" later. I don't anguish over a decision in those areas as much as I do about wasting or not getting the full use from something – like the light fixture.

I share my story only to stimulate you into remembering your own story and evolvement. I challenge you to *pay attention* to all the events and circumstances in life, whether you feel them as negative or positive.

I have come to accept that if we truly believe that Spirit is in charge, then nothing that happens is by accident. We get to grow and mature with each experience. In addition, listening to Spirit in its many forms gives us the opportunity to act and face each event or circumstance and value it as positive rather than getting upset should it not turn out the way we wanted or what we expected.

Further enlightenment on this topic is provided by Frederic and Mary Ann Brussat from their book, *Spiritual Literacy, Reading the Sacred in Everyday Life*:

> Life is a sacred adventure. Every day we encounter signs that point to the active presence of Spirit in the world around us. Spiritual Literacy is the ability to read the signs written in the texts of our own experiences. Whether viewed as gifts from God or a skill to be cultivated, this facility enables us to discern and decipher a world full of meaning.
>
> "Spiritual literacy" is practiced in all the world's wisdom traditions. Medieval Catholic monks called it "reading the book of the world." Muslims suggest that everything that happens outside and inside us is a letter to be read. Native Americans find their way through the wilderness by "reading sign." From ancient times to today, spiritually literate people have been able to locate within their daily life points of connection with the sacred.

Growth and maturity, for the most part, come from our inner struggles of decision-making. Each of us has an area of decision-making that is challenging. These are the areas we need to scrutinize. Become a connoisseur of your own neurosis – as in my being anxious over not utilizing "stuff" to the fullest, even when it's not for the highest productivity. If a repair job would cost $50 for a professional to do, and your own time is worth roughly $50 an hour, you would not be making the best decision to spend your own three hours ($150) on a $50 job! Remember, ALL THINGS WORK TOGETHER FOR GOOD! But to appreciate that, we must be mindful.

Try to pay attention to the many ways Spirit speaks to us and that will allow you to interpret events and circumstances in a way that works deeper in you and for you. Trust Spirit and pay attention to the callings of Spirit in its many forms. *Have faith to act.* Be courageous in living your life.

What you can do:

First thing to do

Write a brief autobiography based on the information gathered so far, entitled "How I Became The Way I Am," noting what you received from each parent or surrogate caregiver as well as conflicting attitudes/beliefs. (You can write this in outline form, if writing is not your "thing," or you can write it as a story. Example: I am an introverted person. My mother criticized me while my father always pushed me to get involved in sports. I was afraid of failure, so I never wanted to take the risk to . . . .)

How you became the way you are relates to how Spirit has spoken to you throughout your life.

Second thing to do

In your journal, define your version of "My Ideal Elder"

- *What would he/she would look like, act like, be like?*
- *What is he/she doing in life?*
- *Include all your ideals about being an elder.*
- *Include family relations, service work, recreation, exercise, body type, etc.*

Third thing to do

Using your imagination, write what is possible and practical: "Whom I Choose To Be" What do I think is possible for me? What is practical? For example: My Ideal may be going on vacations or traveling 300 days a year, but practically I don't have the wherewithal to be doing that, so it would be impractical for me. Perhaps 30 days would be more workable.

CHAPTER 4

FINDING ANSWERS TO DIFFICULT QUESTIONS

We have been told that there is much value in thanking God for everything, no matter what, that there is a blessing in all events. (I must admit that I have some difficulty with the idea.)

How do we give thanks for the loss from floods, money concerns, children on drugs, health challenges, and so forth? There is so much suffering and discontent in the world and in our lives. Many of these difficulties are happening to "good" folks who are attempting to live lives of right action and right attitudes. Why do bad things happen to good people? How do we deal with our personal and world calamities and *give thanks for them?* This seems to be an unanswered question.

Often, when I have thought about giving thanks for atrocities and sufferings, I shake my head. How can I do it? And then my mind goes to the Holocaust and the exiles from Tibet – atrocities and unfairness. How do we "give thanks" for the person that raped our daughter or the murderer on death row?

Perhaps we don't "give thanks" for atrocities in our lives. Perhaps we give thanks for being able to accept them.

Many years ago my wife Sonya and I were in Jerusalem and visited the *Yad V'shem,* a memorial to the Holocaust. Later, I read a section in Lawrence Kushner's book, *God Was In This Place and I Didn't Know: Finding Self, Spirituality, and Ultimate Meaning,* in which Kushner responds to the memorial's wall-size picture of horror and devastation:

> In the center was a mural, at least as large as the viewer; there are three people: a mother, holding her infant child to her bosom, faces the trench. Just behind her, at point blank range, a young German soldier trains the sights of his rifle at the woman's head, about to shoot. In the background there are clouds and the gently waving, autumn grass of this unnamed Polish field.
>
> If there is a God, where was that God when that photograph was taken? God was there. See, we have a photograph. There is God, over there in the ditch,

> in the mother's terrified eyes, even in the psychosis of the Nazi soldier. There is God, an ashen reality, now almost two generations later, more mysterious and holy than ever. The question is not where was God, but why do human beings do such things? Blaming God not only absolves us but increases the likelihood that we will allow such horrors to happen again.
>
> How could God allow such a thing? Why didn't God do anything? To ask such questions assumes that God occasionally intervenes in human affairs. . . (60-61)

Our difficulty lies in reconciling these atrocities with God, whom we have been taught is good. We can relate these questions to the biblical story of Job with all of his trials.

Instead of interpreting the Bible literally, try looking at the people depicted as representational of aspects of ourselves — aspects such as our human capacity for rage, jealousy, piety, self-righteousness, and other character defects. (The "seven deadly sins" come to mind: pride, envy, gluttony, lust, anger, greed, and sloth.) And, if Job represents our human aspects, then God represents our spiritual aspects: the part of us that "knows" – a higher knowing, the Truth. In looking at the Book of Job, try interpreting the Bible metaphysically, wherein each person, place, and event represents an aspect of our own evolution, our unfolding consciousness. Job was certainly a good person and had some terrible things happen to him. He was pious, praised God at length, had wealth and a large happy family. He was a pillar of the community. He did all the right things, a model person.

The story goes that God was holding Celestial Court and the angels, *along with Satan,* attended. (Metaphysically, Satan simply represents another point of view.) So God was honoring Job's good works and casually asked Satan what his views were. Satan chuckled and said that he doubted Job's piety, saying that if Job lost all his possessions, he would curse God and be as disrespectful as anyone else and stop praising God. Satan went on to goad God into giving him permission to "work" on Job. (Note: God is clearly in charge; it is God who is giving permission.)

Soon, Job is robbed of all his wealth, yet he continues to praise God. Then Job's children were killed in a freak accident. But even that didn't deter Job from honoring God and singing praises. Finally, Job breaks out with ugly skin rashes that ooze and are painful. Job, true to form, accepts this calamity as well, and continues to praise God.

Three of Job's friends (Eliphaz, Bildad, and Zophar) heard about Job 's misfortune, and came to comfort him. They all sat for seven days and seven nights in silent meditation. (The Bible is full of "sevens" and the best interpretation that I glean is that of completeness and perfection, as in God made the world in seven days.)

After the meditation, Job came to a different level of truth, a kind of completeness for himself that opened up his inner feelings, and he began cursing his life and cursing God. On and on he went, ranting and raving, expressing his anger with God – very different from before when he was praising and thanking God. (Meditation can bring us to greater authenticity, a perfection that we sometimes interpret as not spiritual.)

At this point Job's so-called friends began to criticize him and pleaded with him to change his attitude and appeal to God. But Job was so angry that he didn't want to hear them. Job's interpretation of all that had happened to him was that God was punishing him. He wanted a hearing with God in order to speak out against his oppression.

God, in His beneficence, granted Job his hearing, and Job lambasted

God with questions of "Why? Why?" He yelled at God, and in essence said, "I have been pious and have praised you with a full heart. I have been a good man and have been repaid with personal calamities."

God responded gently, not by answering Job's questions, but by pointing out to Job his ignorance, telling Job what a nerd he was, that he didn't have a clue as to the workings of the universe.

Being told by God that he was ignorant shocked Job into a different awareness. (Sometimes that is what we need to wake up: a shock of some kind.)

Job realized that God knew exactly what was right and in deep humility acknowledged his own ignorance. (Magic happens when we humble ourselves.) Soon after his remorse, Job's fortune was restored, he went on to have more children, and he lived happily to the ripe old age of one hundred forty years, according to the Bible. (There are many instances of exaggeration in the Bible to get the point across.)

Job believed himself to be innocent of any wrongdoing, undeserving of punishment from God. By this reasoning, we could also say that the Tibetans did not deserve to be exiled, nor did the Jews and many others deserve to suffer and die in the Holocaust. By changing our perspective of judging these calamitous events as punishment sent from a higher power to perceiving them instead as adversities that have always occurred in life, then we will have reached Acceptance.

The way I see it, Job's suffering helped him reach emotional honesty – what we now call authenticity. Job was a righteous man and did good works, but how authentic was he? His truth was covered up by what he thought was "right action." But when he meditated, the truth of his feelings of anger was evoked. By being out of touch with his anger over the calamities, I doubt that Job could have experienced the

Presence and Power of God. If he had been able to know that Presence, then Job's attitude would have been different before meditation.

Job found it easier to blame God than to face his own ignorance. In this way, he could sidetrack any search for self-responsibility to find Inner Truth. Most of us are inclined to blame God or others in our lives when we doubt the good that can come from even an adverse experience: the loss of a job, difficulty in a relationship, money or health problems, or whatever. All events in our lives can lead us to greater understanding and greater compassion.

If we truly understand the nature of God (or Spirit), there doesn't have to be blame. We accept each experience as part of our own growth. I think Job had become complacent and had closed his mind to new thoughts and ideas. The closed mind is ego-driven rather than spiritually driven. In this ego state, the mind is stating that IT knows best, it is not consulting Spirit or anyone. Negativity freely takes over and shuts God out.

Job was expecting God to keep the status quo of his good life. He was simply doing things to keep in God's good graces. His beliefs about God as a Santa Claus who rewards and punishes brought about a dependence upon a false God—the God of his fantasy—not Reality.

I believe this is probably one of the greatest lessons from Job: When we allow ourselves to believe in a remote God, we create suffering. The cause of all suffering is a sense of separation from Spirit, and conversely, a sense of oneness with God (Spirit) brings us peace and harmony.

Pain and suffering may simply be a method that is useful to wake us up to change, be it an attitude, a behavior, or just something that isn't working any longer for us.

When I was divorcing my first wife, the mother of my children, I struggled about leaving the children. Although I was deeply unhappy with my marriage, I loved my children and had some awareness of what our divorce might do to their emotions. It was a very real and painful struggle. But something that I call Spirit kept urging me on, and I proceeded with the divorce. God was not telling me to seek a divorce; I was listening to my inner Spirit and being true to myself. My children were so confused with the messages they received from their mother and me that my two older children found it very difficult to even be around me. I lived with the hurt of my children's rejection of me. I suffered in thinking I had done the wrong thing. The subsequent divorce from my wife and the estrangement of my children had been painful, but I learned acceptance in realizing I could control neither my children nor my former wife. All I could do with my children was to be present and demonstrate to them the love I had for each of them.

I had once suffered terribly over leaving my children behind when I chose to follow my own truth by getting divorced. Keeping in touch with Spirit also kept me in a position to be supportive and loving of whatever problems my children subsequently experienced. Ultimately, the relationship that my children and I came to share has grown to mutual love and respect. Spirit acts on levels beyond human comprehension. We need to remember this when we are "in the pits" and resistant to something that has come into our lives. We can begin to look at our calamities, pains, sufferings, and health challenges as gifts that will help us make some new choices in our lives, thereby moving us closer to a consciousness of our Oneness with God. We can try to remember that God is in all situations, and that most growth comes from our willingness to "get off our position" and consider other perspectives, other ways of living our lives and realizing who we are—A PART OF GOD (Spirit).

A friend of mine who died recently from AIDS used to tell me, "Life is either Recreation or Education."

What you can do:

First thing to do

Recall the times you have said, "Why me? Why me?" throughout your life and record them in your journal.

Second thing to do

Write in your journal how your "wake-up calls" to do something different or to change a life direction were either ignored or acted upon.

Third thing to do

Notice now how each of these calls was necessary to shape the person you have become, and record that in your journal.

CHAPTER 5

QUESTIONING OLD BELIEFS

In my early years, I was quite scientific. I needed to be shown. I had to have proof about what would work—not surprising since our education teaches us to be skeptical until shown proof. Empirical evidence seems always to be required.

My graduate degree from college was in exercise physiology, with an emphasis on scientific data to prove that one exercise, activity, or sport was better for cardio-vascular fitness or conditioning than another. The scientific method was the vehicle that made things believable. If an event could not stand up to this method, then it was considered unreliable.

For an entire year I prepared for a vegetable garden. My son returned to Napa and fine-tuned the drip system he had installed the previous Thanksgiving. During the winter I began putting in a drainage system, building raised beds, bringing rich top soil in for the beds, getting a small garden shed, setting up a compost system and composting with worms. I put down gravel to cover the clay soil around the beds, so I wouldn't be walking in mud. In other words I had a plan and prepared everything just right, so there would be enough vegetables for the whole of Napa Valley.

I was so cool—I had scientifically determined most of what I was doing.

I was prepared. The physical setup was perfect, with drip-watering systems in place. I went to a local nursery and purchased $40 worth of various seeds and special little trays to germinate the seeds. I read all the directions. I made labels and pasted them on the trays to show what seeds I planted in each cubicle. I had a scientific plan, and I followed it very precisely.

So, I planted my little seeds, placed the trays in the front window box to get sun, then – because I was planning to leave for a trip – carefully explained to Sonya how to water them because, as you know, it is quite difficult to place water in a tray!

Everything was perfect—I had scientifically engineered this whole project. When I returned from my trip, the seeds had germinated and were growing. This was very exciting for us both, and naturally, I appropriately praised Sonya for her expert watering technique.

Also, I had a plan for which beds I would plant the different vegetables so the vine type would hang over the edges and the bushy ones would be in the middle. I then prepared to plant them in their beds.

I looked at my labels to determine where each plant would be planted, and guess what? They had all faded to blank from the sun, so I didn't have a clue which vegetable was which; my best scientific plan had been foiled. I am not certain what Spirit had in mind for me to learn from this, but this much seems clear: with all my scientific wisdom, I still had been unable to plan for every event. So I planted the seeds and did the best I could with placement, but I didn't have the foggiest notion of what was what. Want to make God laugh? March firmly ahead with your own plans without consulting God. What a sense of humor.

This scenario gave Sonya and me a hearty laugh—maybe that was the whole point—to laugh at myself. Keep a sense of humor about plans, as well as an open mind. I think it is important to plan but also to be flexible as to the outcome. The process is more important than the result.

The point I'm making is that there is something beyond science that makes everything work. Science can't explain intuition or why a seed grows into life when given warmth and water. Yet the questions we ask are important — not so much for the answers as for the process of attempting to obtain an answer. It is this very process of getting to the answers that mature our minds.

Perhaps science will prove how it works one day. But, for now, keep asking questions and keep seeking answers for yourself. That IS the scientific method for those of us on a spiritual path. There IS a balance between Science and Spirit even if we can't always see it immediately.

When I first encountered meditation, I was still in the mind-set of the scientific method. In the beginning I just went through the motions because no one gave me any proof of what meditation could do. Probably at some level I "knew" that this practice would help me live more harmoniously, help me achieve balance in my life, help me make wiser choices from a more authentic place – because I got quite caught up in meditation, but my conscious mind didn't. My conscious mind had no understanding of this practice, but my unconscious mind seemed to pick right up on it and helped me to stay motivated in keeping with the practice.

As I continued my practice and became more involved with spiritual and religious readings, I became aware of the split in thinking between science, where nothing was believable unless it stood up to the rigors of the scientific method, and Spirit, where experience became the believable.

Then I began reading articles and books by contemporary scientists who were coming up with data that seemed to confirm many spiritual tenets. This was revolutionary for me because I saw that the gap between Science and Spirituality was lessening. Still, there were many die-hards who continued to accept only that which could be proven through science.

And then religion was asking us to believe, citing their interpretation of scripture as valid proof of their position. Remember, a position is a stance that one takes that makes it difficult to allow new information or data to enter which might upset the embraced belief or position.

I find that we do that—we take positions because of "whatever," and then it is difficult for us to move beyond that position for fear that we may appear uncertain or look unfavorable in some way – the all important *ego.*

Then there is Spirituality, which is the essence of belief in life—our own experience!

Spirituality undoubtedly is the basis of various religions practiced in the world, but then soon became a human "position" with dogma and rules, etc. So, spirituality, as I use the word, is a mystical consciousness.

Scientists perform experiments and then tell us what is true from their findings. Mystics discover for themselves what is true. They are explorers, and they use experience as their teachers.

I think most of the great contemporary scholars, thinkers, authors, and scientists have come to similar conclusions in their work regarding spirituality.

My discovery of the following mind explorers contributed to my understanding the difference between religion and spirituality.

David Bohm (1917-1992), quantum physicist, is noted for his underlying theme of life in his book, *Wholeness & The Implicate Order*, he put forward that there is an "unbroken wholeness of the totality of existence as an undivided flowing movement without borders." Existence is seamless, whole, unbroken, and yet passive, and there is a definite order to all of life. This means that everything is connected in one way or another. He further postulates a choreographer is needed and the choreographer is the "self." He says, along with other scientists, that "we" are a process and that *we are science.*

(Interesting idea – that God is our Being and is a part of our process and consciousness. Maybe it's the same thing.)

Aldous Huxley (1894-1963), a consummate scholar who is best known for his writings, is most exemplified by his popular anthology entitled *The Perennial Philosophy*. This work is a grounded source for those interested in understanding Spirit. The essence of his writings is that religions from the Fifth century forward are rooted in a basic truth that all humanity is ONE. We are all related in the human family. However, many religions have *pieces* of other truths that need to be expanded upon. *The Perennial Philosophy* makes the claim that what is within us is also outside of us and what is outside of us is also within us. At the core, we are all united. There is a unity between all religions and spiritual teachings. When we pare away cultural trappings, unity is revealed.

Norman Friedman (1937 -), a highly respected scientist and author of *Bridging Science & Religion,* offers consciousness to Einstein's "equivalency theory" which states there is a relationship between mass and energy. This means that all existence is a form of consciousness, a seamless whole.

Ligia Dantes is author of *The Unmanifest Self* (unconscious self). Her ideas add to the acceptance that Transformation is in nature itself—in the Universe, in the energy that is eternal. She believes in the Oneness of humanity and postulates that *a major method for transformation comes through exploration of one's own inner wisdom.*

Due to conditioning, we experience life as separate entities; however, if we truly experience our oneness, we would see ourselves as all of humanity rather than as the individual "me." Dante states that we are existing in a mostly "unconscious consciousness," and, as such, we have not been able to truly "live life." We would need to gain the awareness of everything teeming with life's energy around us. We can know this consciously. Our "unmanifest self" (unconscious self) can know this spontaneously in a flash of insight or intuition – just a very clear "knowing." Rather than simply waiting for this spontaneous flash, we are invited to explore our inner world to give attention to thoughts, actions, feelings, coincidences, hunches, or impulses if we are to gain confidence in our inner wisdom.

Peter Russell, author of *The Global Brain,* suggests that our planet is a living organism and that it is a part of something larger. He summarizes his hypothesis as the Gaia Principle, meaning that all parts add to the life of the whole planet – animals, plants, rocks, and other matter. Everything is interconnected. Uniting us is a oneness with all of creation rather than a separateness. We humans are linked together through civilizations. All humanity, in the big picture, functions as "one." We are linked mind-to-mind and soul-to-soul. We are a "global brain." If we accept this theory, then we are asked to think, Be, and be conscious in a new way. Our boundaries are less solid and we can begin to experience our oneness. Inner self-growth can create global unity. Personal development and process IS evolution. "Love thy neighbor" is not an admonition but a state of consciousness.

This oneness with the rest of creation rather than the separation of the individual presents a difficulty in attaining this new model —not the constraint imposed by the external world, but the constraints of our own minds.

In the awakening self, there is a need for new thinking. Each cell relates to and influences the other. Intellectual awareness says something is wrong. The Ego says "change the world rather than change self."

As we develop universal compassion, life becomes one of service to humanity and the entire world—all parts ecologically.

Global catastrophe roots itself in a dualistic self-model. Albert Einstein challenges us with the notion that, "Our task must be to free ourselves from this prison by widening our circle of compassion to embrace all living creatures and the whole of nature in its beauty."

To attain spiritual resonance, we are invited to shift from Ego domination to the Universal model. To achieve that goal, we must support inner self-growth for global unity. When the cultural trappings of religion and spiritual teachings are pared away, unity is revealed. We are all united at the core. Our quest for understanding needs to give way to inner evolution.

We cannot understand Reality. God can only be experienced.

We are process beings opening to the whole of existence. We are *becoming* (because we are evolving). We are *process.* We are *energy.* We are a Path unfolding.

We seekers know that we are more than this physical body. There is need for exploring the synergy between our outer and inner worlds, including the mystery of the Cosmos.

We can develop or strengthen the reality that we truly are all ONE. We can begin to replace judgment with discernment. After all, we are partners in the creation of our reality. We can learn that our process allows us to *sin,* that is, make errors, miss the mark. Since we are perfect in our imperfection, we can learn to accept Self the way we are. We are becoming, and we are in process. We can learn to be gentle and kind to ourselves as we discover and learn more about our integral part of all creation.

Ken Keyes, Jr., personal growth leader and peace advocate, wrote *The Hundredth Monkey*, a theory of spatial communication. This particular phenomenon is said to have occurred on an island off Japan where sweet potatoes were dropped by airplane to monkeys below. When one young female monkey decided to wash the grit from her sweet potato in a nearby stream, she passed on the trick to her mother. Soon, all the females were washing the grit from their potatoes. Eventually, they were able to teach the young males to do this "trick." When the last male monkey (in a tribe of 100) washed his sweet potato, an ideological breakthrough occurred: colonies of monkeys on other islands began to spontaneously wash their potatoes. When there are enough folks in one area doing the same thing, that learning is transferred to others in distant places!

It seems obvious to me that all of these scientists and explorers are saying essentially the same thing in different ways and concluding what spiritual seekers and mystics have been saying for eons. Namely, that everything living on the planet relates to everything else thereby creating a balance, or as Peter Russell concludes, "a global nervous system."

The popular premise for people is that there is separation—from each other - from God—from anything and everything outside of ourselves. And the appearance of that seems real. I am here and you there!

The baby separates from its mother! The sun and moon are up there and I am down here! God is somewhere and I am here!

These all are apparent separations. Spirit has always taught us that everything is ONE with all creation rather than separate. And now scientists are reaching the same conclusions.

Ken Wilber is a current modern-day philosopher and scientist who, in one of his significant books, *Sex, Ecology, Spirituality: The Spirit of Evolution*, sums it up succinctly by concluding that science is not only discovering spirit, but validating spirit.

We are challenged to cease thinking that we are in charge—to "let go" and trust that there is a power that guides us, and is greater than the scientific method. When we think we are in charge, Spirit comes along and confronts us. A great many people will think they are changing toward unity when they are merely rearranging their prejudices. BE ALERT. Personal development and process IS evolution. Open the heart. Enlightened people meet Center to Center. "Love thy neighbor" becomes a state of consciousness rather than an admonition.

What you can do:

First thing to do

For three days, become an observer of how all things are connected – to you, to one another, to all beings, to everything. Note in your journal.

Second thing to do

Ponder your current beliefs – about science, religion, whatever. Are you merely "rearranging prejudices," or are you opening your mind? Explore how you arrived at these beliefs. Question whether the beliefs are still valid in your life today. Journal your questions and findings.

CHAPTER 6

MOM & DAD

Mothers

For many years, psychologists, and those that speak the psychological jargon, have felt it was socially acceptable to blame our mothers for everything from colic to mass murders. The premise was that if "the problem" stems from neither a virus nor bacteria, it must then be maternal in origin.

Still others deny all dysfunction in the family and paint this wonderful saintly picture of motherhood that most women have never experienced but continue to try to emulate.

There were three mothers who were bragging on how well they raised their sons. The first mother said, "Oh, my son is a very wealthy attorney, and for my birthday he gave me this gold ring."

The second mother, not to be outdone said, "Well, my son is a very well-to-do medical doctor. He sent me to the South Seas on a cruise for Christmas.

The third mother said, "Well, my son sees a psychiatrist every week.

He pays $150 per hour, and guess whom he talks about for the whole time?"

Many of us have feelings of love and life-affirming emotions about our mothers and that's wonderful, particularly if you were raised to be all that you could be. Be grateful.

But if we have unpleasant memories, what do we do with those memories? Do we free them from where we had buried them years before? Or do we continue to carry the weight of those buried memories around with us?

For years I carried around with me the pain of how I was raised: the confusion, the guilt productions (my mother was a guilt-producing machine).

"I" didn't seem to matter—what I felt and thought didn't count—only her feelings and thoughts mattered. POOR ME! Much of the time I felt I was "in the way." I recall my mother being upset with me a lot and, of course, I was to blame for her upset. Therefore, to keep peace I had to admit to some wrong-doing and apologize to her; otherwise she would pout, and I would feel guiltier than ever.

As an adult, I blamed my mother for most of my areas of weakness, such as my attitude about money, the ways I pretended to be so she would be proud of me, and my concern with appearances rather than Truth. As I began to look less fearfully at myself, it wasn't difficult for me to interpret how I developed two strong patterns of dis-ease that I had: feelings of being wrong a lot and feelings of never quite being good enough.

I had been taught, as most children are, that I was supposed to love my mother, and mother was always *Right* and always *Good.* She was purported to be my best friend—no one could be a better friend. Ugh!!

This put me in a terrible bind because how I really felt wasn't the way I was supposed to feel. I wanted to keep blaming her for the patterns in my personality that I didn't like. It always seems so much easier to blame others than to accept responsibility for who we are and how we act. We keep defending our precious ego position.

I've spent many hours beating pillows—pretending they were mother—and finally, processing my anger and resentment over my upbringing during years of psychological and spiritual work that has changed the way I look at things.

I remember coming across this statement years ago: Life is a series of events that we have created or attracted to ourselves. They just are—unless we judge them bad or good, or blame them for something in our life. They are neutral until we decide otherwise.

I am reminded of a baseball story. A pitcher had pitched three balls and two strikes and was determined to strike the batter out. He pitched the last ball and yelled, "Strike." The batter looked at the pitch he let go by and yelled, "Ball." They both looked at the umpire, who said, "It ain't nothing till I call it something."

The events in our lives are just events until we call them something. Then, we usually become the prisoner of the something we call it. The events in our lives do not stand in our way, but rather our judgments, interpretations, or perspective of them.

From Wayne Dyer's book, <u>You'll See It When You Believe It</u>:

> The belief that others should have treated us differently than the way that they did is, of course, the ultimate absurdity. The universe is always working just the way it is supposed to, and everything in it, even the things that we have judged wrong, improper, cruel and painful for us and others.

In our hearts we know that our mothers did exactly what they knew how to do, given the conditions of their life. It is only our perspectives, our attitudes, and our intentions that determine how we interpret events.

In my years of study, self-searching, and therapy, I have come to an understanding that *acceptance* in life is key to joy and fulfillment. In fact, acceptance has greater value for me than forgiveness. With God in charge of all events, there is nothing to forgive, only to accept. We can learn to develop an attitude of acceptance and learn from each event and circumstance.

The truth is that my mother always loved me to the day she died. I had not been able to accept her for who she was. I had wanted her to be different, to give me exactly what I thought I needed. My experience of having to apologize and swallow my pride helped me to be more humble and own my "stuff."

When I learned to admit when I was wrong and was able to apologize, even the negative turned out to be positive with a change in perspective.

Fathers

As I think back on my growing-up years, I sometimes feel betrayed and cheated. I lost my childhood. I was made to learn the locksmith business when I was seven. Dad was prideful that he could put me on a streetcar, and I would go clear across town, remove locks from the door, and bring them back to the shop. He would then teach me to change the combination for a new key by taking the lock apart—filing and re-aligning the pins, then putting it back together again, and return to replace the locks.

I envied the other kids on the block getting to play ball after school and on Saturdays. I had to go to work with Dad. His intentions were certainly honorable and in line with his time and culture. I've spent many hours untangling the attitudes of my father, deciding what was mine and what was his.

In growing up I remember just wanting to be successful. I wanted to be on top of things, earn money, have a solid relationship, and be happy. My mother's idea was for me to become a doctor, lawyer, or accountant, while my father had no use at all for formal education. He simply wanted me to keep busy by working and learning a trade.

Yet when I wanted to take up a musical instrument, I was told I wasn't good enough and would soon quit. It would be a waste of money and time.

I grew up with conflicting messages. Each parent told me in different ways to be a king, but that I also did not have the ability—not in those words, but that was the message I heard.

I so wanted their approval, and was so frustrated because I couldn't satisfy them both. So what did I do? I grew up with a lot of self-doubt. Still, I do have many positive and loving memories of both of them.

Now I am a father (and grandfather), and I am sure my kids have mixed emotions about me and have their "Dad stories," yet I feel I did the best I knew how for them. I am also sure my parents felt they had done the best with me.

We all have our stories and memories of our parents—and some are very positive and others not. It is difficult to honor and love when there are buried feelings that *feel* not loving.

My attempts to sort out the messages from my mother and father brought about an interesting result. Although on the surface my parental content seemed different, the messages were variations of the same theme—"Be successful, but you are not smart enough." I was a combination of the confusing messages from both.

So many of us don't have a gut reality of our oneness with God/Spirit. Most of us "know" intellectually, but don't really feel our oneness. We separate ourselves from Spirit. This tendency to separate ourselves from Spirit probably goes back to the beginning of patriarchal times.

In patriarchy the God attributes of Father/Mother became separate – sort of like my attempting to separate the messages from my mother and father.

Originally God was perceived to be energy, with no name assigned to that energy. The Hebrews used the letters, YHVH, for God. The first two letters YH meant Transcendent and the

VH meant Immanent — as above, so below. The word could not be pronounced, purposefully, in order to demonstrate the mystery and endlessness, but the meaning was understood.

Because we people need a name and explanation for everything, eventually a W replaced the V. We called God *Yahweh.* To this day those of the Jewish faith don't write the name of the sacred – they use G-d for God.

Even with today's mystical teachings and gender-inclusive language, many of us find it difficult to transfer the meaning of God to an invisible genderless intertwining Spirit/Energy/Principle.

We have been conditioned by Race consciousness, a memory from all time that is encoded in us which Carl Jung called the collective unconscious, to think of God as HE — FATHER — KING.

Many of us became uncomfortable with that male identification of God and began to shift our consciousness to something unifying – something with no gender, no duality, and no separation from God. In just that way, I began to see how both my father and mother cannot be separated within me. They are one within me.

Jesus expresses it clearly when he says, "the Father and I are one," perhaps meaning that the male/female energy of Spirit is one within him.

We males and females may be more alike than we care to admit. And we may create separation or blame with our attitudes of duality. Sam Keen in his book, *Fire in the Belly*, writes of holding his infant daughter and feeling love, warmth, and softness. These are attributes assigned to women. But he contends, and I agree, these are just as much masculine feelings as feminine.

On the other hand, courage, strength, and power are usually assigned to men, although these traits are as much feminine as they are masculine.

We are as much products of our culture as well as of our parents. And many of us have blamed either father or mother or both or some parent substitute for all our negative behavior patterns. Our parents become our scapegoats. They raised us the only way they knew how. They didn't start out with the conversation saying, "Let's see how miserable we can make this kid," or "How can we best screw this kid up?" They did the best they could with the level of awareness or consciousness they had. And while I certainly would have appreciated more support and encouragement, I'm sure my children would have preferred it differently, too.

When I was searching out the Eastern as well as Western traditions, I delved into a variety of religions and met Chilean-born psychiatrist Dr. Claudio Naranjo. With his direction, I explored numerous spiritual teachings, read books, did psychotherapy, learned meditation, etc., etc. Claudio introduced me to the Hoffman Quadrinity® process of psycho-spiritual integration, a method of looking at early conditioning provided by parents or surrogates. I discovered patterns in my life that were limiting my ability to love and to feel whole. (For further reading on this process: *No One Is To Blame: Freedom From Compulsive Self-defeating Behavior*, by Bob Hoffman.) And after all that reading, all that study and work with Claudio, I concluded that *it was all my parents' fault!* I blamed them for everything.

So my first action step was my AWARENESS. My parents were to blame. It didn't matter whether it was true or not—THE WILLINGNESS TO BECOME AWARE, to be honest about my feelings, attitudes and thoughts – is all that mattered. I think this first step (awareness) is the ground or basis for our spiritual evolvement.

Anyway, realizing that they were to blame, I became angry, resentful and hurt. All my negative emotions about them that were hidden from my conscious mind surfaced. I dredged each feeling up one by one to confront them squarely. It was scary for me to look at those feelings because parents are "sacred cows." Motherhood, apple pie, the American flag – these are all part of our formative factors and we keep any negativity about them deeply buried until they are difficult to face at any age.

So, after becoming AWARE that all my problems were caused by parental influence, I lived with that negativity for years, and for the life of me, I could not understand why any person, particularly a parent, would do the things I was accusing mine of, to cause a child so much hurt.

In order to reach some understanding, I needed a framework to help me. I decided to put myself in their shoes: using their life circumstances – from their childhood to parenthood – to see if I could grasp how they got to be the way they were.

UNDERSTANDING became my second action step.

Then, using my creative imagination, I imagined each of their early childhood experiences with their parents and came to a deeper understanding of their reality –they had been children struggling to grow up learning what their parents and the cultural environment of the time was teaching them. By really looking into their lives, I had finally reached a greater understanding of my own patterns and feelings. The process helped me understand that the human condition puts us all in the same process.

Having gotten to this point, I became willing to FORGIVE them for the things I had thought were negative as I was growing up.

FORGIVENESS is the third step. Forgiveness cannot occur before reaching understanding. Forgiveness is touted by most as the way to our salvation, but I don't think we can "will" ourselves to forgive. Such an undertaking of "will" would be mechanical and intellectual, not emotional. Emotion is the substance that makes forgiveness real and lasting. True forgiveness comes from understanding. This process can't be rushed.

When Peter came to Jesus and said, "Lord, how often shall my brother sin against me, and I forgive him? As many as seven times?" And Jesus said to him, "I do not say to you seven times, but seventy times seven." (Matthew 18: 21-22)

It takes as long as it takes until we emotionally feel forgiveness. Seventy times seven may be only the beginning. When we become aware, arrive at understanding and sincerely do our spiritual work, reach forgiveness, then we arrive at the fourth step: COMPASSION.

Having achieved understanding and forgiveness for my parents, I then experienced compassion for their struggles in life.

My mother had escaped the Russian Revolution at age sixteen, and had come to America as a bewildered teenager after losing most of her family. (No wonder I felt bewildered much of my life.) My father was the product of immigrant parents and began his family during the Great Depression.

I became aware. I understood. I forgave. I nurtured compassion.

Then I reached a whole new level: ACCEPTANCE.

If we truly believe that Spirit is in charge, then how can any behavior by any one of us be viewed as a detriment? Instead, every behavior and every action is an opportunity for us to become more aware, to learn from, and to grow.

So, I offer this idea as something to meditate or ponder upon.

Awareness can lead you to Acceptance, and Acceptance will have shown you a new way, a new perspective, allowing you to eschew resentments and blame, negating any need for forgiveness.

I think that through compassion we learn to truly love through our spirit.

We are advised from so many sources to forgive if we are good folks, or spiritual. If we have gone through the four steps outlined (Awareness, Understanding, Forgiveness, and Compassion), then we have reached that transcendent level of Acceptance. From this level, we can truly see that Forgiveness is actually a Judgment. We put ourselves in a position of right or wrong – creating duality. Someone "did us wrong," we believe.

It's Acceptance we need to aim for. All people are doing exactly what they think is right. It is only our perception that we've been wronged – even those who nailed Jesus to the cross. It is the experience that we are/were supposed to have. The question is: What can we learn from each experience? And how can we change our mindset from resentment, anger, hurt to that of Acceptance and Love? I think that is what Jesus' message was, anyhow.

Not that we may not feel those emotions, but we can have a wider vocabulary of understanding and change our self-talk of judging or being wronged to Acceptance. If there are two ways to feel, why not choose the one that uplifts?

As I think back on my locksmith experience, I realize I was critical and judgmental of my father, but I learned much about life that I have used. Besides discipline, I learned that in order to change, I needed to look at what is inside and realign myself for a new way of being – similar to changing the combination on a lock by filing the pins. I think we can learn from all experiences, no matter what.

When we hang on to resentment and anger, the vindictiveness gets anchored in the tissues of our body and restricts our physical and emotional freedom. Life is too short for that; the wake-up calls are happening all around us. We don't have time for negative thinking or the harboring of resentments that can limit our loving and our freedom.

Not too long ago my father decided to dance with the angels. Losing a parent or early caregiver usually brings up or touches some very deep feelings. At an early age that person actually was our thread to staying alive. No matter what kind of baggage we have with a parent, we feel the loss when death claims them.

Since my mom died over ten years earlier, I had taken Dad under wing and attempted to be more attentive than when he had the companionship of Mom. As a result, Sonya and I took him to Israel and Egypt when we went prior to Seminary. He turned out to be a real trooper – hiking up hill and dale to see and experience all that he could while in our company. We took him on a cruise to Mexico, and I spent a month traveling with him up the West Coast, stopping at his grandkids' homes to visit. We paid him lots of attention, and in the process we became quite close.

Ever notice that when you spend time with someone, arguing, laughing and loving that bonding happens? Well, that's the way it was with Dad. We grew closer than we ever had been and shared much with each other. During the several months before he died, he visited us, and he was so pleased that we had found a location we loved. We had moved around so much, and that was unnerving to "PaPa." But we took him around as we were looking for a home to purchase when the Unity Church Board decided to hire Sonya as its permanent minister. Dad was so pleased with us finally settling down; he said that he had a certificate of deposit that was maturing and that we could have it to help with our down payment. We were delighted and thrilled to get that help.

When we finally found a home we liked, I called him to tell that we would need the money before too long. He told me that he rolled it over, and it wouldn't be available for nine months. We were devastated! It was difficult for me to express what I felt because Dad was getting older, and I was concerned how he would take what I had to say. Nevertheless, it was important for me to communicate my feelings, and I did this in a letter.

He became quite upset that he had inadvertently locked up the money. He didn't think we were that ready and he was so sorry. We both shared our feelings and there was nothing more to do. We both felt terrible. And it all worked out where we were able to purchase the house anyway.

During the next months his health deteriorated, and I went down to Los Angeles and spent a week with him in the hospital where we talked a lot. We began to heal years and years of hurts and misunderstandings. We talked about death and its mystery, and we talked about life and its mystery, and about God and that mystery. It was good. We shared lots of love. I returned to Los Angeles to spend another week with him before Christmas, and we grew even closer with our intimate communication and expressing of emotion.

We talked about him coming up to be with us for a while and he was considering that. After twenty-seven years in the same apartment, this would be a big step for him. We were excited about the possibility of his coming to live near us, so we could have quality time with him during his declining years.

Perhaps depending on others for his care was too much for him, and he decided it would be more beneficial to be with the angels. The day after Christmas, he sat down in his chair and died peacefully.

I was glad he hadn't suffered much. He had managed to be with the family for Christmas, and he indicated to us that he felt complete. I am blessed to have had the time with him that I did and, even with all the old "stuff" I had with my father, I recognized all the good he was and what I had been taught for my life.

We can let go of any misgivings with our parents and truly surrender to God's love and move on with our lives, no longer held back by limited behavior conditioned by our parents. We can do this with the power of will, or free choice. (When I did my own work around my parental upbringing, I also practiced a meditation I learned at the Hoffman Quadrinity Institute. This meditation will be included in *What you can do* as the Fifth thing to do.)

What you can do:

First thing to do

Become willing to be Aware – about your true feelings, attitudes and thoughts – regarding a challenging person in your life. Note these feelings, attitudes, and thoughts in your journal.

Second thing to do

Reach Understanding by putting yourself in the other person's shoes. Try to see this other person's behavior from that person's perspective. Imagine the difficulties this person may have had in life that would contribute to his/ her outlook or behavior. Journal your growing awareness of being in another person's shoes.

Third thing to do

Forgiveness actually evolves through reaching Understanding. Because this is an evolving process, this state is not usually achieved immediately. No good purpose is served by feeling guilty because you don't reach Forgiveness in an instant. Allow this to occur. Continue to journal your evolving thoughts and feelings.

Fourth thing to do

Out of Forgiveness, Compassion will walk right in and take up residence in your heart and mind. Journal this new state of being, what it feels like, how you got there. With the realization of the Compassion you now have, you will begin to see that you now have Acceptance. Journal this new energy.

Fifth thing to do

(Instructions for GUIDED MEDITATION: By reading the following guided meditation into a tape recorder, then playing it back, you will be taken through a simple meditation process that can be very powerful. It is a process of accepting our parents or parent substitute and the parents within us. This process can change your life. This meditation can be modified to use with any relationship you want to heal.)

Prepare by expelling a couple large exhales, and then by observing both the "inhale" and "exhale" breaths. Notice how the belly rises and falls. Notice the temperature of the air as it flows in and out of your nostrils.

Be comfortable – feel the chair supporting you – there is nothing to do but breathe. Feel yourself let go of tension and holding (check your body, your jaw).

Allow your eyes to close – feel that you are in a place of ease and rest, breathing easily.

Allow your creative imagination to reach a mind-to-mind communication using the higher spirit of yourself and the higher spirit of your parents or parent-substitute. Use a biological parent or parent that raised you – whether on this physical level or in Spirit level.

GUIDED MEDITATION:

Imagine/ sense/ see/ feel your father/ mother/ other in front of you – the part of those parents or substitutes that had only love for you – the part of the love with which they fathered and mothered you.

Look into their eyes: first one parent, then the other. Imagine (see, feel, sense) their caring. Make it up if you don't feel it. Create the feeling you wanted!

Hear each of them saying to you, "I raised you in a way that I thought best for you; I wanted you to be the best you could be."

Hear, sense, feel them tell you, "I am proud of you my son/ daughter, and of what you have become. You have been a good son/ daughter." Imagine that first with one parent, then with the other.

"We know that we did things that may have hurt you and limited you, but we did the very best we knew how and meant only good for you. We didn't know what damage it would cause you in your life. We know you may be angry and hurt for some of the things we did, but please know that we love you and have always loved you. Find it in your heart to understand and accept us for our intentions and love for you."

Stay with the energy for a moment. Say to each parent separately:

"I ACCEPT YOU TOTALLY. I UNDERSTAND. It may take my human self a while to integrate this understanding, but I will do it." Then, imagine them thanking you and all of your higher selves; they and you reach out and embrace. Let the emotions happen.

A healing and acceptance has been done on the spiritual level. Let it work for you!!

- - -

When ready, open your eyes and return awareness to your surroundings.

You might note how your family and others treat or respond to you or you to them. You might note if your life begins to change with your friends and family. And you might keep in mind from this point onward to accept all events and circumstances that come your way, and to look at each item in a way that teaches you something. Be aware of the way you respond or react. Each situation can assist in your maturation and help you live your life fully.

The Jesus story begins with the message, "He is blessed and one with whom his Father is well pleased." Repeat to yourself: "I am blessed and the Spirit within me is well pleased."

CHAPTER 7

REDISCOVERING FAITH

Deuteronomy 6:4- 5: "Hear 0' Israel the Lord our God is one Lord, and you shall love the Lord your God with all your heart, and with all your soul, and with all your might." This passage is known as the great commandment. The book of Deuteronomy summarizes the Israelites' forty years of hard wandering in the wilderness, led by Moses following their release from Egyptian bondage.

It was during this time that the people were enticed to create and worship a graven image of God. The Israelites were severely scolded by Moses for this act, and so they gave up their golden idol.

But as they approached the Promised Land, Moses knew he would not be entering with them, and he was fearful that they would return to the worship of false gods. If people knew God the way he did, idols would be unnecessary, and they would then be prepared for the 'good life' in the Promised Land.

How many of us love that energy that is God (Spirit) with all our heart, soul and might? Or are we often like the Israelites wandering in the desert and worshiping the graven images of money or other peoples' opinions?

My wilderness times have been when I become hassled by the conditions of everyday activities: taking care of the children, dealing with decisions at work, or being unhappy with the way things are going in many of my relationships. This may be hard to believe, but the hardship comes from us, not Spirit.

If we change our minds about our expectations, then the way we feel can change too. What I've learned is that all I need to do is follow the Great Commandment: Love God (Spirit) with all my heart, soul and might.

When first going into the Unity School Ministerial Program, I found myself continually studying, and I began to feel hassled about all the work. I didn't know what to do. I prayed for an answer; then, I listened. I came to the conclusion that I was not living a balanced life, which to me meant that I did not love all of me. I needed to love all of me because Spirit dwells in me.

When I discussed it with Sonya, we concluded that the imbalance was that my playfulness was being neglected. My life was mostly schoolwork. I guess that's what happens when we dedicate our lives to something. We focus so intently and become imbalanced.

I turned inward to explore my thoughts and feelings. I learned that I was frightened of not being 'good enough.' So I changed my mind about what 'being good enough' meant to me, then I began to have more fun. Had I not listened to what was happening in my life, I probably would have continued to feel hassled.

When we are still and listen, the One Presence and One Power guides us through our indwelling Spirit. The answer could come in a second or in forty years. There is no time limit on when Spirit answers us. It is the *process* that will prove to be important.

Chasing the Carrot

Sometimes we are not still, and we don't listen because the human mind is both wonderful and insidious. It can come up with glorious ideas and inventions that benefit humanity, and it can send us chasing after false and wasteful things. One minute we may be immersed in creativity (in touch with our Spirit within), the next we may be judging whatever it was we created, telling ourselves how inept we are, how untalented, how useless or hopeless (disconnected from our spirit within). Intellectually, I understand the futility of that disconnectedness, the futility of attacking myself or sending myself chasing after unrealistic expectations of perfection. Most of us past middle age learned long ago to stop doing that to ourselves, and then, much to our own surprise, catch ourselves in the very act of judging ourselves negatively.

What a poor inventory is negative judgment alone. Any store would close down if it could not balance its liabilities against its assets. If a store inventoried only liabilities, you could expect to see an "out of business" sign on its front doors. I kept thinking about this when I caught myself in one of these hectic chases after the impossible, and what I finally realized is that occasionally I seem to worship at the wrong altars: Ego, O.P.O. (Other People's Opinions) or Perfection.

I'm no different than those who came before me. In the Bible, Baal worship was the worshipping of other gods. In fact, the First Testament of the Bible contends that all problems and wars are the result of Baal worship. Essentially, it is the loss of connection with our god or spirit within.

Moses, the staunchest advocate of worshipping one god, Yahweh, was livid when he returned from the mountain top with the tablets of the Ten Commandments only to find his people had created a golden calf to worship. In his rage, he threw the tablets down, destroying them. Jesus experienced a similar frustration with his people when they willfully refused to understand his teachings.

Throughout history, various populations have worshipped multiple gods, assigning to each god some aspect of life: gods of war, peace, love, farming, fertility, et al. Historically, then, humans have found it difficult to worship and trust an invisible God, a shapeless and formless energy, no matter how powerful. We looked instead for something we could visualize – an image or icon of some kind. Most of the western world settled easily into an anthropomorphized version of God. We made God in our image – an old man with a white beard who sat on a throne somewhere above the clouds and looked down upon us.

The truth is that we were made in God's image, not the other way around. Yet, in our world today, we are still worshipping gods that seem more real to us— money, sex, power, to name a few. When I doubt myself and indulge in negative self-judgments, it's the same thing as not trusting God, putting my trust instead in a God of Doubt.

Sometimes I see myself (and others) as the proverbial donkey that has a pole attached to his bridle that dangles a carrot not far from his nose. The donkey keeps chasing but never reaches the carrot. We keep chasing and never get what we really want. In my own history, I chased the carrot in many ways. During my athletic coaching days, I chased the power and recognition carrot. Once I had achieved the correct amount of power and recognition, then I would feel fulfilled, content. The empty feeling would be banished. However, that didn't happen, so, during my business days, I chased the money carrot. Well, surely the right amount of money would do the trick. And when that didn't work, I launched myself into self-improvement and began a spiritual quest. I chased the teacher carrot, seminar after seminar, training after training – one of these teacher carrots would give me what I needed.

There is a story about God and the angels shortly after the completion of the world and all its inhabitants. God mused to the angels one day that He would have to find a place to hide so people would not see Him. One of the angels suggested that God go to the farthest reaches of the universe – that people would never find Him there. But God said, no, His people were smart and would one day find ways to travel the universe. Then another angel suggested He go to the depths of the ocean where it was too dangerous for people to go. But God said, no, His people were smart and would devise machines and cameras that would scour the depths of the ocean. The angels then pondered this perplexing problem but could find no suitable solution. God suddenly shouted, "I've got it! I'll hide inside each of them. They'll never think to look for me there!"

If we seek fulfillment and can't find it in our achievements, our successes, if we think that someone else will give us the answer, or that if we only do the right thing we will be graced with fulfillment, then, at least we are seeking. The search itself indicates that we are on a path. The fact that we knock on all the wrong doors along our way is only human. Eventually, we stop seeking that which is on the outside – the carrots – and begin to go within. The deeper we are willing to search within ourselves, the greater the likelihood that we will discover the God within.

Are we likely to keep getting sidetracked? Certainly. In Matthew 7:15, we are warned to: "Beware of false prophets who come to you in sheep's clothing but inwardly are ravenous wolves." Whenever we give our energy, our power, our knowing over to someone or something else – a book, a teaching, a minister, a religion, or whatever – we are idolatrous. Instead, we can be discerning. We can determine for ourselves what best serves us without giving up our power and energy to the false prophets. The Power is within us.

Most of us have been taught to put our trust and faith in Spirit. Why is this so hard? The problem, as I see it, is that many of us are not willing to put the energy into developing a personal relationship with Spirit that could develop our faith and trust. How do we create a personal relationship with an invisible God? The same way we create a relationship of any kind: by taking time, hanging out, conversing, sharing, becoming willing to sit still and listen (in other words, prayer and meditation). If we remain unwilling to spend our time and energy in creating this relationship, then God remains an intellectual idea and not a personal reality.

The story of Jesus and his Temptations

The temptations came to Jesus after his baptism during his 40 days and nights in the desert wilderness. Opportunities were presented to him that offered pure worldly gain and personal recognition. These temptations pushed him to the limit of his faith. Ultimately, he resisted all of them.

Would it have been possible for Jesus to go through those trials without the discipline of keeping his focus on God? Through his intention and willingness to say NO to the seductions, Jesus created the freedom and strength necessary for his ministry. This was an aware and conscious choice.

When we consciously choose, we feel in control of our lives—no matter what the result of the choice.

However, consciously choosing (by prayer and/or affirmations) doesn't guarantee the outcome will always be to our liking. There has to be something else. That something else is DISCIPLINE!

Like Jesus, we have to keep our eye on the goal with disciplined intention to move us through those temptations that limit our freedom. We can't merely *think*, "God is in charge of my life, so I don't need to sit and pray or meditate daily. Since every thought is a prayer, I'm in continuous prayer."

Well, we'd be half right. Every thought *is* a prayer. And are we fully aware of our thoughts all the time so that we'd want these "prayers" to reach their destination? God may be in charge of our lives, but God also gave us free choice. We may be given intuitive thoughts on how to act in a given situation, but in our free choice, we might just ignore that intuition. If we make it a habit to pray and meditate on a daily basis, we increase our odds that we will be in tune with that intuitive thought, that God-connection.

"But I prayed and meditated yesterday; why do I need to pray and meditate today?" Because, today is a new day. Each day is a new day – a gift to us. Perhaps that's why we call it "the present." We discipline ourselves to pray and meditate each day, and prayer and meditation become our discipline – the very thing we need to master the circumstances of our lives.

Bible stories show us that our struggles and doubts, our temptations to take the easy way out, are nothing new. The stories remind us that this human behavior has been going on for a long time before we came into the picture. We are all tempted to serve and follow other gods in their many forms, to have faith in something tangible (career, relationships, money, power) rather than something ephemeral and mysterious. Jesus had to struggle with his temptations, as in Matthew 4:8-10:

> Again, the devil took him to a very high mountain, and showed him all the kingdoms of the world and the glory of them; and he said to him, "All these I will give you, if you will fall down and worship me."
> Then Jesus said to him, "Begone, Satan! for it is written,
> 'You shall worship the Lord your God and him only shall you serve.'

Master the Elephant

In *Prayer: The Master Key,* by James Dillet Freeman, there is a tale of an elephant:

> A student was listening to his master discourse. "All is God," declared the Hindu guru. "And God is the infinite, the one, the only, without limitations, without attributes. This is the essence of the wisdom of the ages. This is the beginning and the end of truth."
> The student, sitting at the feet of his master, drank in the words in all their heady essence.

"I understand," he exclaimed, "God only is real, and reality is only God. God is one and God is perfect, unaffected by external circumstance. He is everything that is. He is the reality within me. He is the reality within you. All things are only the forms through which He expresses Himself."

As the student left his teacher and walked down the road, the truth that he had just imbibed seemed so real to him that he felt intoxicated. In the flowers by the roadside, in the beasts in the fields, in the birds that flew overhead, in the human beings who passed by, the student saw only God.

Absorbed in this sweet bliss of divine illumination, suddenly he saw, coming down the road, an elephant. As the huge beast lumbered swiftly toward him, the student could hear the tinkling of the many bells that dangled from its harness. He could hear the soft thud of its great feet on the road. He could hear the voice of the elephant driver perched on its neck, who shouted, "Clear the way! Clear the way!"

But the student thought, "Why should I get out of the way of this elephant? I am God. The elephant is God. Should God be afraid of God?"

Full of faith and without fear, the student kept to the middle of the road. But when God came to God, the

> elephant, at a command from the driver, with a quick twist of its trunk hurled the student headlong into the ditch.
>
> After a while, dirty, bruised, and shaken – even more shaken in mind than in body – the student crawled onto the road, limped back to his teacher, and poured out his tale of pain and doubt.
>
> "Ah," said the teacher when he had heard the student through, "You are God. The elephant is also God. But why did you not listen when you heard God's voice calling to you from the driver, who is also God, to get out of the way? (230-232)

In your life, are you in the driver's seat, or are you standing in the road speaking affirmations, praying, repeatedly thinking positive thoughts while telling yourself that the Elephant is not going to run you over? Suddenly in our lives we are confronted with the elephant – illness, relationship stress, finances, job insecurity, troublesome children or parents.

In desperation we usually turn to prayer, asking God to resolve our dilemmas with the outcomes we outline. And when God doesn't do exactly as we have asked, we wonder why prayer doesn't work. At this point, many of us go back to the books, the teacher, the minister, and even to God to demand an answer to what went wrong.

Life! Isn't it interesting? We think we have a handle on things then, all of a sudden; the elephant comes along and upsets our equilibrium by throwing us in the ditch of discomfort in dealing with some life issue.

As Freeman says,

> . . . the Elephant does obey. It obeys the one who is in the driver's seat. It will not do what we want it to do because we think lofty thoughts or speak magic phrases. It will not turn aside because we are mystics or because we are good people morally. It will not kneel because we have absorbed the contents of a book on metaphysics. But when we have established our authority over it, it will obey us, not because we compel it, but because its very nature – the very nature of the universe – compels it. (232)

Sonya and I wanted to give my daughter and her husband a time-out from the children, so our two young granddaughters — Jenna and Hannah — stayed with us. What an experience for us both after not being with that age group for so many years.

When I noticed that Jenna had been dictating to her younger sister how to use a particular toy, I came in to tell Jenna to not interfere with Hannah. Jenna resisted my instruction and continued to attempt to control her sister. Hannah, in turn, was resisting Jenna's controlling behavior and wanted to do it her way. I found myself becoming upset that I was being ignored. I became angry and began scolding Jenna, who ran off crying. Later, after I had cooled down, I realized how reactive I had been. It was really none of my business. The problem was theirs to work out.

Now I think I am a fairly evolved person, yet I found myself sinking to the two–year-old's level, and the awareness of my reaction made me ill. She wanted her way and, of course, I knew best and wanted my way. As I made this gradual awareness, I realized that I was the one out of control. So I thought about it and decided to talk to Jenna about my feelings and allow her to tell me how she felt. I told Jenna why I had gotten so angry for trying to control her sister — how I had thought it best for Hannah to play with her toy the way she wanted and not the way Jenna wanted to dictate. I then apologized for butting in, and told her it was not my business, but between her and her sister.

Jenna listened attentively and seemed to understand. We understood each other, and then everything was okay between us.

I had explained my reaction to her as I would another adult, and respected her as a person. We no longer had to engage each other for power. There was such a great transformation of attitudes, and what a great learning for me. This system works for adults the same way—communicate with and respect each other.

Her behavior pointed to MY elephant (control—my way) and I learned how to master the elephant and become the master in myself. Until that mastery happened inside me, I was in a power struggle with a two-and-a-half-year-old. Did I feel dumb!! My granddaughter, in turn, wasn't in the tension of trying to please an adult on the one hand, and satisfy her self-exploration on the other. She was a happy camper, and so was I – a real win-win situation.

Freeman summed up: "The student was not wrong in his insight into the nature of things, or in his faith that he did not have to be afraid of the elephant. He was wrong in not realizing that before he could master the elephant, he had to become the master."

Some folks want to command the elephant (like my wanting to feel good and be in control in the presence of a screaming kid). Perhaps the elephant could be our teenagers not listening to our wisdom, or simply when life is not working for us the way we expect or want.

I had to resist the conditioned way of responding to a child and become a master of my emotion before the idea could come to me as to what to do. Only then could change happen.

Are we able to say no to the habits and patterns that don't work for us anymore? Say no to our own addictions? No to negative thinking? No to people who want to invade our lives? Are we able to master the feelings that are going on inside us?

I find that so many of us continually distract ourselves from the inner work by engaging in a variety of activities and/or looking for ways to be entertained. Often we look for someone or something else to make us feel uplifted and good.

Distraction and entertainment can be good things, but if we are to live conscious lives, then it would be helpful to be conscious about our choices. I know that most of *us* make conscious choices, but I'm talking about those other people! I know for me it takes a great deal of energy to stay conscious and be aware when I am running from myself or my hurt, rather than dealing with a negative pattern I am attempting to avoid. I must admit that I am not always successful.

Instant gratification seems to be the disease of our time. Take a pill for fast relief from discomfort. Buy a lottery ticket and become a millionaire overnight. Brush your teeth with this special toothpaste and become irresistible to the opposite sex, or the same sex. We have been conditioned for the "quick fix."

So how do we get into the driver's seat and learn mastery? When I mention the word *discipline*, see what that word stirs in you. What emotion? Meaning? What thought? What came up for you? Hard work? Stupid repetition? Parental authority?

I know that for many of us the word Discipline brings up lots of stuff. Many people have been abused in early life, so the word translates to punishment.

Here are more words of wisdom. From Proverbs 5:23: "He dies for lack of discipline, and because of his great folly he is lost." From Hebrews 12:11: "For the moment all discipline seems painful rather than pleasant; later it yields the peaceful fruit of righteousness to those who have been trained by it."

Although controlling ourselves may seem like punishment, it's really only our taking charge. Discipline, then, gives us our greatest freedom. Discipline, I have found, is the path to mastery.

George Leonard, a modern mystic wrote,

> True fulfillment comes not through climaxes but through mastery: the process of returning again and again to a discipline or task, sticking to your work even when you appear to be going no where (sic—like in meditation). The discipline can take many forms: it applies to even such mundane pursuits as dish washing or vacuuming. It allows us to live more fully in the present moment.

Truly, if we are to become master of the elephant, we need discipline.

Ask some musicians how they got to their level of excellence. Hours and hours of practice—practice—practice. When I decided to learn how to play the guitar (as an adult), I found the experience to be downright painful because mastery of the instrument came so slowly. My fingers didn't move fast enough, and my musical memory was lacking. I was embarrassed to tell anyone because I thought I should be able to play a tune or something by now. I began to make excuses for my inability, and several times I just quit. Yet I have disciplined myself to practice daily even through the feelings of frustration. I began to see some improvement, and that alone is a miracle and worth all the practice – the discipline.

The quick fix is seductive, but it is never enough; we always need more, and as the philosopher Eric Hoffer stated, "You can never get enough of what you really don't want." The inspirational or informative talk, a truth principle, a high climatic event may contribute to the feeling that our lives are working, but unless we follow up with disciplined action, that feeling is usually short lived.

Set aside a regular time to practice your art, your music, your drama, your craft, your prayer, your meditation, because that is what is likely to reward you with your greatest freedom.

By serving Spirit, we serve ourselves best. The carrots of Money, Power, Sex, and the Easy Way Out are simply false prophets and hollow idols. We waste our time, energy and talents by chasing them. Make a commitment to sit still, and with prayer and meditation begin your relationship with God/ Spirit. In this way we get in touch with the powers that are truly ours. (See Chapter 11 for more on these powers.)

What you can do:

First thing to do

To experience that "feeling of control," think of three things you feel you are unable to accomplish with any skill. Write those things down beginning each sentence with "I can't ...." Whatever it is you feel you "can't" do. (For instance, at one point I believed that "I can't" play guitar.) Now read aloud what you have written. If typical, your feeling should be that of a victim, or a very young orphan child.

Second thing to do

On another sheet of paper, write down the same three things, only this time begin the sentence with "I won't." Read aloud what you have written. Your "feeling" might now be that of an older, rebellious child ("You can't make me, you can't make me").

Third thing to do

Now, on another sheet of paper, write your three items beginning with the words, "I choose not to ..." When you read these aloud, you may notice that your feelings have shifted and you feel like an adult – no longer the victim, no longer the rebel-

child, but an adult in charge of your own life, controlling your choices.

CHAPTER 8

THE WISDOM IN PRAYER

Some, but not all of us, know that there is value in prayer. In our scientific age, we often question the validity of anecdotal and personal experience as related to prayer. Dr. Larry Dossey, in *Healing Words: The Power of Prayer and the Practice of Medicine*, reports solid, scientific, controlled-experiment results showing that prayer can influence bacteria in a laboratory dish or the relapse rate of coronary patients. But the studies hold a surprise for us. Some studies have included two prayer strategies: directed and non-directed. In directed prayer, the person praying attaches a specific outcome to the prayer – for physical healing or for some other measurable and desired result. In non-directed prayer, the one praying does not specify the desired outcome. The pray-er simply asks for the best to occur in the particular situation – in other words, "Thy will be done." The outcome is left for Spirit, God, Christ Essence, the Divine Mind, Love, or Higher Power, to decide. The studies show that both approaches are effective, but that the non-directed prayer is more powerful. Some researchers suggest that non-directed prayer works better because there is an inherent perfection, wholeness, rightness in the world that manifests itself if all obstructions are removed. If this is true, then we need not tell the universe what to do because God is ready to do what is best for us. We call this Divine Order.

Nevertheless, I don't want to set a formula for prayer. Each of our efforts to interact with God (Spirit) can be unique and honorable. If directed prayer works, then use it in the ways and situations that seem right to you. There will be times when you will be led also to non-directed prayer. Trust your feelings.

Masaru Emoto is a Japanese researcher who has written *The Messages of Water.* Some of Emoto's conclusions have been published in the periodical, *The Spirit Maat,* (Volume 1, August 2000) under the title "Conscious Water Crystals, The Power of Prayer Made Visible," by Susan Barber:

"Emoto has been conducting worldwide research on the effect of ideas, words, and music upon the molecules of water..."

Photographs accompany this article that make Barber's words and Emoto's research more vivid. In referring to one of these photos of frozen water samples showing what seems to be an amorphous blob, she writes: "After the above water sample had been taken, the Reverend Kato Hoki, chief priest of the Jyuhouin Temple, made a one-hour prayer practice beside the dam. After that, new water samples were taken, frozen and photographed . . . the change is stunning – the ugly blob of the former sample has become a clear bright-white hexagonal crystal-within-a-crystal."

A third photo of a frozen water sample " . . . of water taken from Fujiwara Dam after the prayer treatment, reveals a shape that had never, prior to that time, been seen by Masaru Emoto in his over 10,000 water-sample experiments." The photo depicts a heptagon, or 7-sided crystal.

Emoto's research with frozen water samples led him to claim that:

- *"Water from clear mountain springs and streams has beautifully formed crystalline structures, while the crystals of polluted or stagnant water are deformed and distorted.*
- *Distilled water exposed to classical music takes delicate, symmetrical crystalline shapes.*
- *When the words 'thank you' were taped to a bottle of distilled water, the frozen crystals had a similar shape to the crystals formed by water that had been exposed to Bach's 'Goldberg Variations' – music*

composed out of gratitude to the man it was named for."

After witnessing Emoto's startling photographs and research results, Barber speculates that " . . . we can begin to really understand the awesome power that we possess, through choosing our thoughts and intentions, to heal ourselves and the earth. If only we believe."

These studies bear out what mystics have known and many religions have taught through the ages. Prayer is essentially communication with Spirit. So, how do we pray?

What you can do:

First thing to do

To begin, consider that there is an intelligent, benevolent power in the universe. Align yourself with that energy; remembering that the true purpose of prayer is to change us or our attitude, not to change God or God's mind. Prayer is one way for us to achieve acceptance. Directed prayer can be called affirmative prayer. Our prayers are not beseeching God to do something for us – not, "Dear God, please get me that new job." Rather, our prayer might be something like, "Dear Spirit Within, I affirm and know that the perfect job for my highest good is unfolding for me now. Thank you." That, of course, leaves the way open for us to recognize new aspects of the current job, or to be directed to a career we had never considered before, or to some other quite unexpected outcome.

So, directed prayer might begin with an acknowledgment of Divine Presence, using whatever name you prefer – God, Christ, Spirit, Higher Power, Allah.

Second thing to do

Acknowledge that you experience and know that the power is within you. Then express your need or desire in a positive format. You might say, "Spirit within makes me prosperous now," or "God is healing this relationship now."

(Prayer doesn't have to be complicated or long, nor do we have to resort to the Thees and Thous of King James. It can be very simple – one sentence of plain language. The most important things about prayer are your intention and sincerity. In a way, this kind of affirmative prayer is like non-directed prayer in that it simply reminds us to work with God, rather than demanding that God work for us.)

But true non-directed prayer goes a bit further. In non-directed prayer, we surrender any and all results completely to the will of God. The 13th-century German mystic Meister Eckhart said, "God is willing to give great things when we are ready . . . to give up everything." And as the prelude to the Lord's Prayer states, "Your Father knows what you need before you ask Him." Remember, studies show that merely praying, "God's will be done" has a greater effect than directed prayer. How can we really know, in the truly grand scheme of things, what is best for us? Shakespeare said it best: "We, ignorant of ourselves, beg often our own harms, which the wise powers deny us for our good." Perhaps that is why, in 12-Step programs like Alcoholics Anonymous, members learn to pray "only for knowledge of God's will for us, and the power to carry that out."

CHAPTER 9

LOVE & RENEWAL

We're admonished to love the homeless as well as the affluent and the murderer and victim equally. These are difficult admonitions, aren't they? Yet, the two great commandments tell us to Love God with all our hearts, minds, and souls, and to love our neighbors as we love ourselves.

We probably aren't conscious of all the perspectives on love. We tend to have beliefs about love that we learned in childhood and continued to hold onto, as we grew older.

The Dance of Love

Around Valentine's Day, I am reminded that the love that's usually associated with this time of year is usually endorphin-inspired, a rush of romanticism that really *feels* good.

We all "get off" on this type of rush, and sometimes we look for it in all the wrong places. This feeling, this rush, is usually short-lived because the feelings are really about ourselves. We like being in love. Essentially, this could be called "endorphin-love." Endorphins are chemicals the brain releases that give us a feeling of well-being. Eating chocolate can bring on an endorphin rush. With endorphins, we like "loving."

There is, however, another kind of love that is more lasting and feels pretty wonderful too. This is the kind of love that acknowledges and respects another, that allows the "other" to do and be what is best for that person without demanding – or wishing for –something in return. Most of us want to be "loved in return," and that's a pretty natural wish, but this kind of love acknowledges that desire, becomes willing to release it, and goes on loving anyway.

In the late 1950s, there was a very pretty and talented young movie actress, well on her way toward becoming a major Hollywood star. In the midst of her success and while engaged to a handsome young businessman, she made a decision to relinquish all that she had attained and become a nun. When she told her fiancé of her decision, he was surprised and saddened, but he supported her desire to join the religious community. Nearly forty years have passed since Dolores Hart became a nun. Her former fiancé has never married and still visits her every year, consoled by the belief that their love has sustained itself.

From the romantic love of youth, this kind of love has evolved into something so stable, so comforting, that the earlier desires no longer matter. Although people make decisions to go in different directions, it does not necessarily follow that the love borne for each other will die. This same kind of love is available to each of us, when we can put aside our expectations.

From 1 Corinthians 13:4-7 comes this definition of love:

> Love is patient and kind; love is not jealous or boastful; it is not arrogant or rude. Love does not insist on its own way; it is not irritable or resentful; it does not rejoice at wrong, but rejoices in the right. Love bears all things, believes all things, hopes all things, endures all things.

Love can also translate to understanding, compassion, and acceptance.

Ken Wilbur is a transpersonal psychologist and author of many books. He writes of his wife, Treya, dying, having been diagnosed with terminal breast cancer ten days after their marriage. Not particularly romantic.

Treya had gone through a wide variety of conventional and alternative treatments—from chemotherapy, radiation, megavitamins, meditation, psychic healers, and surgery. During their first five years, there were recurrences and setbacks, and their relationship became stormy. They bitched and complained and wondered what their lives were all about.

During that time of process, they came to understand and to view life from a Buddhist perspective – where everything that happens is taken as an opportunity for serving others. Their relationship became one of each simply serving as teacher for the other, and in so doing, they glimpsed that eternal spirit that transcends both the self and other. Their relationship became stronger as they worked through the questioning and learned compassion for each other.

I believe that COMPASSION is the prelude to LOVE. And these two truly came to a deep love for each other before Treya succumbed to the disease and died.

Real love can hurt! Real Love makes us totally vulnerable. Real Love can take us beyond ourselves and, sometimes, can devastate us. It's been said that, if love doesn't shatter you, then you don't know love.

Ken and Treya learned "spirit" love through their understanding and compassion for each other, through the adversities that life had handed them, not through romantic love.

I learned another translation of love when Sonya's brother in Florida had been taken to the hospital with symptoms of numbness and a seizure; we soon learned that he had a tumor on his brain. Emotionally bottomed out from my brother-in-law, Wayne's, condition, I was, at the same time, in the middle of excitement for the impending birth of my daughter's second child.

In the midst of it all, I attempted to make some sense of it because, after all, I must understand. Oh, boy! I thought about some of the virtues I work with, and one of the most frequently encountered is the virtue of Equanimity: to treat all events and circumstances with some degree of equality. I practice cultivating this virtue, the idea being that emotions and events happening in this world pull me from my "center" and my peace.

These events certainly did that to me. I was in the middle of two extremes. How often that happens to us, doesn't it? Maybe not this extreme, but we get caught between these two poles often.

There is an old Japanese Buddhist story that demonstrates equanimity:

A priest is taken to prison for impregnating a young girl. When the authorities had come for him and told him the charge, his only response had been, "Ah, so." After the priest had been in prison for fifteen years the woman confessed that it wasn't the priest who had made her pregnant. The authorities came and apologized profusely and all he said was, "Ah, so." Either way – that's the way it is. I'm not sure I could respond that way.

I found myself thinking about how we are admonished to love. We're not told to love one thing more than another, are we? We're told to love all persons equally – no matter what their race or color.

And since we Seekers know that God is all around and within each of us, we need to learn a degree of Equanimity by loving. Period.

Gradually, I realized that this meant that the tumor needed to be loved equally as the newborn baby. Rather than turning away from the abhorrent aspect of the tumor, I had to find a way to embrace the reality of it, to accept it with the same love I would have for the newborn child.

Now, that was difficult for me to do. But that is what I learned to do. It was easy to pray for the baby with loving; however, all my conscious awareness was needed to pray for the tumor – that whatever its birth was about that it, too, should be borne out. In my prayers I attempted to create some equanimity. I prayed that both the baby and the tumor come out to fulfill their destiny. I had to learn to love them both, to trust that each would do what was necessary to bring about the highest good.

Perhaps all of us might begin allowing prayer to guide us into whatever action is needed, be it a phone call, a letter, travel, or a strong intention – whatever intuition dictates. We are invited to learn to listen to the "still, small voice" and not be tempted to ignore it because it seems like something that is not really real. The bottom line is that we never know why things happen. The lesson to learn is how to respond to all events with some degree of equanimity and love.

This may seem difficult for some of us, yet if we continually practice, we gain skill.

Attitudes About Love

During my early years, my notion of love was primarily romantic and sexual. I think this notion was (is) probably common for many folks. When I was twenty-one and in the Navy during the Korean Conflict, I married my high-school sweetheart, who was two years younger than I. When my two years of active duty in the military were up, I enrolled in college, and we settled in Santa Barbara, California; our first child was born during my senior year. Throughout my undergraduate study in Santa Barbara and graduate work at UCLA, I pursued the life of the "white picket fence." I believed I was on the right track, and, on reflection, I think I was in my head rather than in my spirit.

By the time I had earned my graduate degree and finally became a coach at a local high school in Santa Barbara, we had three children. Feeling pressured by the need to earn more income, I moved into real estate, where I could make more money for my family's growing needs. Unhappily, although the money poured in, the satisfaction did not. I "awoke" to a very deep feeling of unhappiness during my first marriage and began to question choices I had made. I had begun to realize that "doing" (changing jobs, making more money) was not fulfilling to me. This led me to question what (and who) was necessary for happiness in my life. Years of therapy – for both my wife and me – were simply prolonging an unhappy union.

A colleague in real estate introduced me to Transcendental Meditation, and I tentatively embarked on my spiritual journey. Unfortunately, my wife could neither understand nor support my growing interests, which was the beginning of our painful path through separation and, finally, divorce.

Meditation – many different kinds – and psychological awareness had begun to induce a greater acceptance of who I was and what drove me. I was now in a better position to start making clearer and more conscious choices.

Serenity Prayer

God, grant me the serenity to accept the things I cannot change,
The courage to change the things I can, and
The wisdom to know the difference.

Reinhold Niebuhr

Many years had to pass for my attitudes about love to mature. Like most young people, I *thought* with my hormones and made choices accordingly. As I grew more aware and more accepting of *what is,* rather than the way I thought it should be, I discovered I no longer *saw* people in the same way I once had. I began to see what lay within the person, rather than the surface attractiveness. To my surprise and delight, I found myself more and more attracted to that quality of authenticity that may not be immediately apparent to the average viewer. This personal authenticity became more seductive and alluring than an hourglass figure. My attitude had gone through a transformation. In fact, attitude is the one thing we can have control over when we gain awareness and learn acceptance. Our attitudes are one aspect of ourselves where we can acquire the courage to change.

I have read many definitions of love – both literal and spiritual, yet each seems to fall short of describing this emotion, this state of being. I have come to the conclusion that trying to define love is like attempting to define God, spirit, or the wind. What we can describe is the *effect* that love has. For instance, we are not able to see the wind, yet we are able to see – and feel – the effects of the wind. We can see leaves stir softly on a tree when a breeze wafts through its branches. We can feel its gentle caress on our skin. The power of the wind can be enormous, bending trees to the ground during hurricanes, pulling them out from their roots by a tornado. Love has the same quality of mystery and power as the wind. We can't see it, either, but we can see and feel its effects. Love can dispel loneliness. When love has been absent for a time and then is allowed to enter, the effect is like that of an anemic person receiving a transfusion. Warmth and life flushes through that person, and the evidence of love having entered is visible, although love itself cannot be seen. Love is an experience; it is beyond words. Only its effects can be described. But to truly understand love, one must experience love.

I am not suggesting that divorce and mid-life go together. What divorce stimulated for me was the evaluation of what was missing in my life – my awareness of a spiritual connection, along with the behavior patterns that unknowingly had been controlling me.

A spiritual context had been absent, as well as a relationship that was open enough for my partner not to feel threatened by my thoughts and feelings—or for me not to be threatened by another's thoughts and feelings. I had to grow up. More importantly, I now wanted to grow up.

The process of reviewing my life, as well as my new practices of meditation and spiritual study, all assisted my changing attitudes about what I wanted in a relationship. Since I had discovered that my presentation of myself had not been authentic, but merely as I thought I should be seen, I realized I yearned for authenticity. During the years of being single after the divorce, I was quite lonely. I had awakened to some deep awareness and had made some corresponding changes, but some of my old attitudes were still intact. I still believed that having a physically beautiful woman in my life was important. So I would discount being with anyone whom I judged didn't match the image I wanted to project. Obviously, not many were up to my standards; I was quite lonely. As I became more aware of how arrogant I was and what ego-driven motivation was running me, I began to look at relationships differently and became more open-minded regarding the appearances of others. I began dating and hanging out with women who were more "real" and not necessarily attractive when measured against my old standards. I discovered a wonderful new beauty. As I allowed myself to be with all sorts of folks, I began to see beauty all over the place.

In the beginning, I had to consciously push myself to relate in order to be with some people and found the true gold when I let go of my preconceived ideas. People are people, and they are all beautiful once we expand our perspectives. The depth in most folks can't be realized unless we are willing to *be* with them and to just let them *be.*

I went through several relationships during those years following my divorce. In each one I learned a bit more about myself, and my ideas about what would sustain a long-term relationship began to change. I began to see that I must be willing to be "hurt" if I was to have an honest, open relationship. In other words, I had to be willing to hear what my partner feels and thinks even if it appeared to be negative toward me. If she spoke about having a sexual attraction for someone else or found another more stimulating, I needed to be strong enough in my own right (to have enough confidence in myself) that those words wouldn't allow me to cave in. Just because my partner has those feelings doesn't mean she will act on them. But we need to talk about them or they will get stuffed into some dark corner of our psyches and will come out in other ways that could be detrimental to our relationships. These everyday experiences and commitment to compatibility are the keys to healthy relationships.

Throughout our lives we are usually dancing between romantic (or endorphin) love and "spirit" or compassionate love. Parents, teachers, spiritual leaders, songs we hear, and books we read – all encourage us to love. The scriptures of all religions and philosophies tell us to love. We know that loving is the right thing to do. We just don't always know how to go about it.

So, these steps of Awareness, Understanding, Forgiveness, and Compassion can and do lead us to Acceptance, to a place where we become more loving – even to those for whom we don't care that much. (See chapter 6)

These action steps can assist you to better understand and love your partner, your friends, your children and even your enemies. We can ultimately learn Giving to Give rather than Giving to Get.

My study with Bob Hoffman, founder of the Hoffman Quadrinity Process who developed this four-step action process that teaches us how to love with our spirit – a process that may evolve to that love that has no expectations, only acceptance. (These steps may seem obvious, but it took me a while to put them together to learn them.)

What you can do:

First thing to do

(This is a meditation I like to use. You can read it into a tape recorder and play it back):

Relax your body and breathe deeply. Put your left hand over your heart and your right hand over the top of your left. Just sit there for a moment and feel any love or sensations that arise in this position. While still in this position, begin to think, and feel the idea of love and what that means. LOVE from the heart. (Pause.)

Fill yourself with that love. See and feel yourself as spiritually fulfilled. See your partner, your significant other, or your best friend fill with that love and that same spiritual fulfillment. (Pause)

Expand yourself by extending this love out to all friends as well as those who are challenging. Just imagine them, or feel, or think them. Make this an intention. Keep expanding. Extend the love, thoughts, and feelings to your spiritual family, the community, the greater community of the world, and foreign countries. Dare to love everyone equally and intend all peoples to reach spiritual light fulfillment. Feel it, work with it, and learn to live it. Entertain the idea of Equanimity of love.

Second thing to do

Here you will use information gained from the questions "Who hurt you?" and "Whom did you hurt?" from the "What you can do" section of chapter 1. Look at your part in these transactions. Surprisingly, this exercise will empower you, not diminish you. It will be necessary for you to make amends to anyone you have hurt, unless to do so would cause further injury. If the person is no longer alive, amends may be made during a meditation where you can ask for forgiveness; this becomes a mind-to-mind communication with our "high selves." When meeting this way and asking forgiveness, forgiveness is automatically granted. Suggestions for performing this meditation may be found in Chapter 6, Mom & Dad.

CHAPTER 10

QUIETING THE MIND: THE WISDOM IN MEDITATION

Transformation comes by doing our inner work with intention. In Hebrew this is called *kavannah.* The strength of intention is important and will dictate the time you need to devote. The process of mastery is finding your way to learn and then to practice in daily life with *kavannah* (intention).

Sometime ago I talked to someone who was feeling like he was in the ditch. So I asked about his spiritual practice, and he said he usually sits a few minutes quietly, praying to God for help, then does a couple of affirmations. I gathered that the whole thing took about five minutes. That was his spiritual work. He probably thought that worked for him, but judging from the results, something else was needed for him to pick himself out of the ditch. It's not that any of those things are wrong or even that the time spent was too short, from my perspective. We need whatever amount of time that we need to quiet ourselves and learn to listen and to enter the sacred space. For me, there is so much inner chatter that it takes me at least thirty minutes to get quiet before I can enter the space.

Meditation is *intention* — disciplining the mind by using a mantra of intention.

One way to still the mind is by using a single point of concentration. Regard the following instruction from Kierkegaard's journal:

> The unreflective person thinks and imagines that when he prays, the important thing he must concentrate upon, is that God should hear what he is praying for. And yet in the true, eternal sense it is just the reverse: the true relation to prayer is not when God hears what is prayed for, but when the person continues to pray until he is the one who hears, who hears what God wills.

In my previous book, I mention that prayer is talking to God, and meditation is listening. The challenge, of course, is that usually God doesn't talk quite as loudly as we think we would like. We have been instructed, as noted earlier, to listen to "the still, small voice." If we train our minds to quiet, to let go of some of the chatter, we have an opportunity to hear the still, small voice. There are many books about meditation, lots of theories and practices, techniques and teachings. All of them have value in some way, and I encourage you to experiment, to see what works for you. I have learned through my own experience that, like prayer, meditation also can be kept very simple. Once again, intention is everything. Time and discipline of practice are needed to reap the reward.

The effect of meditation is a quiet knowing that the universe and we are in union. There is no separation, only a natural rhythm. Any discomfort or psychic pain usually results from having a sense of separateness from the Divinity that seeks to express through us. To be healed and whole is to experience our connection with this Absolute. Meditation helps us to know this truth, to experience it fully. As we experience our true center, our Star, our Christ within, we become more able to act from that center.

We can meditate anywhere, in any body position. Meditation is being mindful of each moment. It is simple, but not necessarily easy. Here are four basic steps: Preparation, Relaxation, Meditation and Thanksgiving.

1. Preparation relates to the environment. It helps to set aside a place that will be used specifically for meditation. That doesn't mean that you can't meditate anywhere anytime, but

most of us find that if we select and regularly use a specific location, our concentration is enhanced.

2. Relaxation means letting go of tension in the body. Sit comfortably. Then, beginning with your feet, bring your awareness up through your body, releasing any tensions you find as you go: feet, ankles, legs, pelvic girdle and genital area, lower back, abdomen, upper back, chest, shoulders, arms, hands, neck, jaw, face, eyes, forehead, ears, scalp. Relax them all, then scan your body once again for any remnants of tension.

This might be a time to practice forgiving anyone that you need to — including yourself. "I forgive the delivery person for knocking over the birdbath," or "I forgive my sister for yelling at me," or "I forgive myself for gossiping about my co-worker, for buying that extravagant meal, for making that mistake."

3. Now we come to meditation practice. Meditation is going into the silence between thoughts. At the deepest level of concentration, thought may cease and just *being* becomes our reality, and we experience the Silence. There are many levels of awareness in the Silence, including what some have called non-awareness, or pure awareness. It is during this time that Divine Mind can speak to us in various ways to suit our needs at the time. It may be an inner-harmonious feeling, an idea, a direct inner knowing, a definite statement or affirmation.

Many of us have learned to evaluate ourselves according to some criteria learned from others. The experience of meditation is yours and yours alone. Each of us is unique, and it is not helpful to compare ourselves or our experience with what we think someone else is experiencing. We tend to think that everyone else is experiencing God or Bliss or Nirvana or something else that we are not, and therefore that we must be doing it "wrong." But there is no wrong way to meditate, except not to meditate. If we are willing to set the time aside for this sacred experience, to keep the intention of our mind on the single focus, then we have done our part.

It might help to think of the mind as a puppy that has been put on a long leash. The puppy begins to wander and explore, as puppies will, until it gets to the end of its leash. When it feels the tug, the puppy returns to its owner at the other end of the leash, becoming aware of its master once again. Some people find it helpful to use a *mantra,* a word or phrase that is meaningful to them and that is repeated continuously in order to reduce random thoughts.

Another approach is to use the breath as a guide. Just pay attention to your breathing, observing the in-out, the inhale-exhale. Or just count your breaths. If you lose count, start again. When thoughts come to you, just notice and let them pass like clouds in the sky. Gently return to watching your breathing. Notice what happens in your body, what moves, the temperature of your breath as you inhale and exhale. In time, your thoughts will fade.

It is a challenge to practice this discipline with no particular goal in mind. However, it is a wonderful adventure. So, just sit and narrow your focus to a truth principle or your breath. That's all there is to it. You might want to do this for ten to twenty minutes in the morning and perhaps again in the evening.

4. The last step is giving thanks. When we are ready to stop our meditation, then it is time to be grateful for each breath and for life. Think of all the things you are thankful for: your family, partner, children, friends, situations, shelter, food, body, and others. Gratitude helps our Star shine as we go back out into the world.

Every moment we practice prayer and meditation, we strengthen our conscious contact with God. As that contact is strengthened, we find it easier to rely on that Presence in all our daily business. We find we know how to handle situations that would once have left us puzzled, upset, or angry. We find that what we need comes to us just as we need it. We discover that we can do things that once seemed totally impossible. We smile more. We shine.

The Labyrinth Model for the Journey of Life

In Chartres, France, the Notre Dame Cathedral stands as an extraordinary example of Gothic architecture. Many visitors to the city come to view the cathedral's renowned stained glass windows and marvel at the warmth emitted by their color and light into the interior. Not so many visitors come to experience the pattern on the floor of the church – a pattern known as the labyrinth. It consists of a large circle with many circuitous paths leading to a smaller circle at its center. To reach the center, one begins at the "entrance" of the outer circle and proceeds along the marked path that, for a time, travels around the circumference of the circle before abruptly turning inward toward the center, then out again.

As one takes the pilgrimage of the labyrinth, one gradually sees that the path turns many times toward center, then outward and back, before finally culminating in the circle's center.

The "pilgrimage" is meant to be a meditative one, and the "pilgrim" may have many experiences or insights while progressing slowly and meditatively upon this journey. Some people have reported that their experience of moving toward and then away from the center, allowed them to *feel* how drawn they were to the center, their momentary disappointment at turning away from it, their gradual understanding that if they simply kept on the path they would be drawn to where they wanted to be.

When several people are taking the pilgrimage, they discover that at first one pilgrim may seem to be following another, only to have the person veer away in an inward or outward direction. Yet, as the pilgrim continues on his journey, he encounters his fellow traveler again, and yet again. As one approaches the center and another is leaving, it is inevitable that they encounter one another side-by-side at some point. This is often accompanied by a sense of timelessness, a tidal ebbing and flowing – the rightness of which seems to permeate the pilgrim. Many pilgrims report a feeling of oneness – a certain connectedness – when they reach the center and remain there for a time. Others report feeling this connection with the other pilgrims, who may even be strangers to them. Some, on this journey, have said they felt slightly lost and unsafe as they moved away from the center during their journey in or out. Even when leaving its center as the pilgrim makes his way to the circle's exit, he continues to weave in and out from the center to the outer. He begins to have a sense of reassurance, a realization that he now knows where "center" is and he can always return to it. Having completed the journey, the pilgrim becomes aware that the labyrinth is a microcosm of the tidal ebb and flow of life.

Selfless involvement in the midst of life is one of the keys that will unlock fulfillment. Reaching goals only establishes new goals. What all of us need is a balanced life. We need to participate totally and yet find a way to escape to our inner silence away from the clatter of the world clamoring for our attention.

Meditation can help us touch those quiet places. Those who meditate have a sense of their inner conflicts and are more willing to work on themselves than those without meditative experience.

In completing the journey to this last phase, we become aware of humility and service—not grandiosity. We recognize that this is our opportunity to pay back to God what has been given during our time from beginning to now.

Breakthrough

What happens when you take the risk to go inside yourself? Usually, you discover that you are not as bad as you had thought – you're not the scum of the earth. You also may discover that you may not be as good as you thought—grandiosity gives way to authenticity. It is at this juncture that you may begin to "enlarge your house." If you had embarked on a decision to increase your living space by adding a second story, you would be dismayed (to say the least) to discover your house collapsing because you had neglected to look for termite damage prior to the remodeling. Personal inventories are just as necessary before we begin the remodeling project of our lives.

Our work is going deeper to the center of who we are. Our willingness to explore and our intentions are what make it all work.

Rumi: "When you have entered the way, God Most High bestows on you kingdoms and worlds that you never imagined; and you become quite ashamed of what you desired at first. 'Ah!' you cry. 'With such things in existence, how could I ever seek after such a mean thing?'"

Getting through to our Center tends to happen over time after an intense experience, effort, or struggle that helps it come to fruition. Knowing when this happens varies from person to person. We experience the great "Ah hah" and know that we know that we know that we know. In that moment of realization we are "awake." This state can happen by grace without any intention on our parts. However, the intention can help make it happen. It is a wonderful feeling when we finally get that sense of knowing that cannot be explained—it is, simply, an experience.

What you can do:

First thing to do

Go on your own pilgrimage. This means that whatever you set out to do today, do it with awareness. The Buddhists call this "the beginner's mind:" being aware of thoughts, feelings, and actions.

Second thing to do

Look – and really SEE – whatever you encounter during this pilgrimage because when you return, you will journal what you have seen and discovered: your TOTAL experience – thoughts, feelings, and actions.

Third thing to do

Review the four steps outlined in this chapter to create your own meditative practice or experience.

CHAPTER 11

THE TWELVE PEARLS: TIMELESS WISDOM

The 12 Powers We All Possess

The Six Thinking & Mental Powers: Will, Order, Judgment, Understanding, Imagination, Elimination

The Six Feeling & Sensing Powers: Faith, Power, Strength, Zeal, Life, Love

Unity is a world wide spiritual movement founded by Charles and Myrtle Fillmore in the late 1800's. Its emphasis is on supporting individuals in their developing inner strength on their journey to a conscious awareness of their oneness with God. According to Charles Fillmore, the "God-mind" has twelve perfect attributes – six thinking and six feeling.

Therefore, the Twelve Powers are a framework that we call upon to help us focus and direct our lives.

The thinking/mental powers are: Will, Order, Judgment, Understanding, Imagination, and Elimination (Renunciation). The feeling/sensing powers are: Faith, Power, Strength, Zeal, Life, and Love.

We don't acquire these twelve powers – we already have them. We have the ability to use these powers all the time. They support and empower us. They are tools to help us achieve balance. We can focus on and practice the ones in which we are weak.

We were born into this world with these twelve attributes. As we grew out of childhood, we began to lose awareness of these powers and how they are active in our lives. Usually, as our egos grew larger, our connection with these powers diminished. Claiming ownership of our twelve gifts – our twelve powers – is part of our spiritual journey. As we feel our powerlessness, we seek power; we search for what is "lost." In reality, the only thing lost is our awareness of what we already have.

Our suffering, frustration, sense of failure, and world disorder come mostly from our misuse or imbalance of these powers. Constructive enlightened understanding and use of our powers leads to "salvation." The word salvation comes from the Latin *salvus,* which means *healing* or *wholeness.*

Think of the word *salve, meaning anything that soothes or relieves. Salvation* or *being saved* means the state of healing or wholeness that comes by allowing Spirit to call forth and direct our Powers.

According to David Williamson, Gay Lynn Williamson and Robert H. Knapp in their book, *Twelve Powers in You,* we are like projectors of Spirit, living from the inside out as we project onto the screen of Life, and Spirit is the sum total of all the Creative Energy in the Universe. Some call this Creative Energy *the Christ.* When I speak of the Christ, I am referring to our innate Divinity or Spirit, not a single man. Others may call this our *God Self,* our *spiritual essence,* our *Buddha nature, Atman, I am,* and/or *transpersonal self.* The Christ expresses in us through our powers of mind. We project our God Self out into and onto *the world* or the *screen of Life.* The Christ, our God Self, is like a light bulb in a slide projector, always shining – not necessarily providing more light, rather improving the quality of our slides (beliefs, self-image, conceptions, viewpoints) and radiating the light more fully (holistically) so we get improved conditions on the *screen of life.*

If we want to change what is on the screen of Life, we don't go out and change the screen, we change what we are projecting ONTO the screen. Since we are the image of God, we are projecting the image of God outward.

Unity minister and author Eric Butterworth believes that some people look at life and say, "What's in it for me?" Conscious people look at life and ask, "What's in it from me?"

One of the ways in which we become sages or wise elders is by understanding and using these powers to balance and to know ourselves. For example, Love needs to have Wisdom and good Judgment to make wise choices. Understanding needs Faith and Life to manifest.

(Some of the metaphors and ideas used in the following definitions of the powers have been borrowed from the book *Twelve Powers in You* by David and Gay Lynn Williamson and Robert Knapp.)

THE SIX THINKING & MENTAL POWERS:

Will, Order, Judgment, Understanding,
Imagination, Elimination

WILL

Will is our executive faculty and is the spiritual power that directs. We are on God's "Board of Directors." When we learn the power of the *will* we can learn how the process of "not my will, but thine be done" works.

We may not work in executive positions; nevertheless, in our own lives we are the Chief Executive Officers. We are all in a partnership with a Higher Power. It is a dynamic and multilevel, multi-national, multi-cultural, multi-racial, multi-everything enterprise. We are appointed and being charged with being the CEOs of our own lives. Our executive power is our *will* power. This is not the type of will power needed to stay on a diet or to stop smoking cigarettes. But there is more to *will* than staying on a diet or stopping smoking. Will is the spiritual power that enables us to make executive decisions and then execute them. We decide and then we do. When we make "will" statements, we are acting as a CEO, and this is the way we cooperate more fully with the divine will. For example: I *will* graduate from school. I *will* have a sense of humor and not take everything so seriously. I *will* be patient and tolerant. I *will* involve myself in positive relationships. I *will* organize and prioritize my life. I *will* do what needs to be done to be a wise elder. I have free choice, and I can choose to reject or accept my good. God's will is always good, even though we may not at first perceive it that way. When we listen closely to the still, small voice, we get the right guidance. Then it is up to us to choose to accept or reject it. Many times we have been operating strictly on the gratification of our own egos, presenting a deaf ear to our inner promptings. And then we wonder why our lives have become so complicated. Our power of *will* needs to be strong and directed by the highest and best in us. This does not mean we impose our will on others.

Most of us have experienced power struggles; they are merely clashes of will. This is a negative use of the power of *will.*

The opposite of being aggressively overbearing is being a doormat and being indecisive. Instead of assertively standing on our own two feet, we allow others to take charge of our lives. In his classic book, *Christian Healing,* Charles Fillmore wrote: "The idea of giving up the will to God's will should not include the thought of weakening it or causing it to become in any way less; it properly means that the will is being instructed how to act for the best."

One of the most challenging tasks for me was to discern my will from God's Will. Years of conditioning and surviving in this world had led me to believe I was in charge of most outcomes in my life. Happily, I have since found that the only thing I am in charge of is my attitude. The faculty of Will has assisted me to continually challenge my attitude and change it when it is necessary. Vigilance is the master key. Will became powerful for me when I felt I had aligned my will with God's Will. I determined how to make this alignment by continuing to make choices, except now I was slowly trusting the choices I made. I learned that my intuition was a message from Spirit, and when I ignored or questioned my intuition, acting instead on second guesses and over-analysis, the results were less than desirable. On the other hand, when I followed my hunches, I was successful more often than not.

When I decided to enter Seminary to become a minister, my decision was based on pure intuition. I had never thought of becoming a minister even one year prior to my choice. The inspiration came in a flash during a breakfast meeting and following through was the work of Will.

We say *Thy will be done* so that we surrender our will to Spirit's will. When we pray *Thy will be done,* we are opening ourselves to become conduits for Infinite Good to pour into and through us out to humanity. So, choice is a key awareness in the operation of *will.*

ORDER

Order is spiritual law. Charles Fillmore, in his teachings of these twelve powers, says that Order is the basis of our "standing alone with God within as our self." Order is within our innermost self. When we follow that inner voice, we are in perfect order. It is when we allow the voices of ego to distract us from our inner listening that we are out of balance and not following the divine order. The spirit within (or God) is everywhere present. There is no place where God leaves off and we begin. This means that God and I are one, and that you and I are one – with God within each and every one of us.

Order is the ability to know what is important, putting first things first. Order helps to establish and maintain worthy personal and social priorities. Our power of Order is mainly concerned with our ability to clarify values.

Helice Bridges of Del Mar, California, tells the following story about a high school teacher in New York who used a process developed by Bridges. The teacher wanted to honor her seniors by telling them how they made a difference in the world. So, using the Bridges idea, she presented each student with a ribbon imprinted with gold letters, which read: *Who I Am Makes a Difference.* One of the young men presented a ribbon to a junior executive, who helped him with career planning. The junior executive decided to give a blue ribbon to his boss, who tended to be a grouchy fellow. He presented his surprised boss with the ribbon, putting it on him and praising him for his astute qualities. This made the boss feel important, that he mattered and that people cared about him. He was given an extra blue ribbon with the request that he pass it along to someone else who would also be affirmed by receiving it from him. So the boss decided to give this ribbon to his teenage son, to whom he had not been paying much attention and who had become increasingly distant. When the boss went home, he knocked on his son's bedroom door. His son yelled through the door, "Yeah?" wondering what his dad wanted. The father came in and said, "Son, I've been busy and occupied with my work and other things. I know I yell at you about your grades and messy room. I haven't given you the love I feel for you, and

I want you to know you mean a lot to me. I want you to have this ribbon because you really do make a difference in my life. You're a great kid, and I love you."

The startled boy began to sob and couldn't stop. His whole body shook. He looked at his father and said through his tears, "I was planning on committing suicide tomorrow, Dad, because I didn't think you loved me. Now I don't need to."

We need to check our values to make sure we are our spending time in areas that are most important to us. We say we love each other, yet we yell at our loved ones over a light that's left on, a broken dish, a scratch or dent on the car. Sometimes we take better care of our lawns than we do our relationships. We spend long hours weeding, trimming, planting, watering, and fertilizing. We lavish a great deal of time and money on our gardens while our relationships dwindle from lack of care.

Every day we say yes and no to many things. It is important to take the time to order our lives and do those things that are important because no matter how full our schedules are, if we try hard enough, we can always fit more into them. But is that what we want: a life crammed with activities? We need time for learning and growing, time for meditation and physical exercise, time to be aware of spiritual values, time to help others to grow and succeed. And we need to let others know how they impact our lives, time to serve a cause beyond ourselves. We need quality times with those we love and who love us. These are the big things that we need to put first, or activities that aren't meaningful at a deep emotional level crowd them out. We need to clarify our values by prioritizing, putting first things first, and creating a positive order for our lives.

The illusion I continually struggle with is the idea that I can establish Order. The truth is that there is a divine order to all things and many times life just seems chaotic. For example: the chaos in my life pushed me into looking at what I needed to do to simplify my life. My challenge was to get rid of the items that were superfluous and look for what would create more order in my life.

I am always looking for a new system to simplify my life and my tasks. I say to myself, "If only I had someone to help me with my files and bookkeeping." So, I hired someone to help me set up a system. I purchased new computer programs that I think will help me with a variety of tasks and interests. Then there is the garden watering system my son created for me to keep watering simple. I added the shelving for the garage so I can have more Order there.

I continually have an inner dialogue with myself as I go through things around the house and garage, finding things I need to give away to reduce clutter around our home. I also have an ongoing inner dialogue about the files I need to eliminate. Some of my files were over thirty years old, yet I had not looked at them once in that time. My original way had been to look at chaos and think I needed to do something to create Order. But things are moving so fast these days that what was Order for me in the past is no longer true today. I needed to change my idea of Order to survive in this fast-paced world. Action is the answer for me. Doing what is in front of me rather than worrying about some Order that I have in mind that keeps me feeling I am never done. Some things in my life now seem like they are out of Order, but I feel great since I stopped pressuring myself to do it the old way. Out of chaos comes order. The Divine chaotic push is what allows me to simplify, but I must be willing to act on the "push." When I experience disorder, I look to what it is telling me and then I can choose to act or not act; but it is the power of Order that is operating. I now feel that there is a higher Order operating in my life, and I continually look for those old patterns that still have the capacity to "run" me and look, instead, to what is fresh for me to do, which may be to clean out my files.

JUDGMENT

Judgment (Wisdom, Discernment) is our ability to discern, evaluate, and make decisions, to "make up" our minds. Heaven and hell are states of consciousness created by the decisions we make, not places we go to after we die.

We become more aware and conscious by listening to our hunches, our intuition, even the occasional or chronic pain in the neck or back or stomach as well as the deep aches of our souls. We pay attention to our dreams and wonder about the tears that come for seemingly no reason at all. We discover, in retrospect, that have we learned something about ourselves when our careers, our marriages, our health, hopes and dreams came apart. Our miserable experiences turned out to have value when our perspectives on these events changed. Just like umpires, we make the calls of our experiences; we can choose to call them in ways that depress us or in ways that lift us. Our perspectives determine our happiness.

We might ask ourselves: what kind of self-talk am I using? We have the opportunity to use our wisdom and judgment to choose a perspective that is worthwhile, healthy, helpful, healing, positive, and peacemaking. When we make these choices *consciously*, we bring balance, harmony, and wisdom into balancing both our heads and our hearts.

During my early life, what “ran” me was being successful, as measured by the money I earned. My ego was concerned with looking good in the eyes of others. I needed to have the prestige of being unique. I believe that these were the triggers of my life. They ran me. I began as a teacher/athletic coach, then real estate broker, then Rolfer, then workshop facilitator and, finally, minister. Each move involved my being able to discern what the move meant. Did it originate from my ego, or was this true discrimination and growth? Now, I realize that each move was for my highest good. At the time, I did not realize consciously that I was discerning and preparing myself to do deeper work. In time, I decided to leave pulpit ministry and focus more on community service, which has included becoming a chaplain for the local police department. In retrospect, the moves were divinely guided through my faculty of Judgment.

Some time ago, my wife and I began a cross-country journey in our nineteen-foot camper/van. Our intent was to travel for a year to promote the book I had just published. I felt successful. My children were grown, and I had a wonderful life partner. Well, you can imagine what happens with two strong people over time in such a small space. Yet, we survived and grew a great deal from the experience. And as we listened, Spirit guided us to a small church in Napa Valley, and after only six months we decided to settle there. The church could not afford two ministers, so the plan was for Sonya to take the position and for me to be free to do whatever was in store for me to do. Yet I had no idea what that would be.

I very much wanted, and struggled for, a clear answer NOW. Yet, nothing spoke to me clearly. I'm still awaiting a clear answer to my Promised Land. And as I travel the country doing workshops and seminars, I find that many others have the same feelings.

I continue to be challenged by what's next because I am aware of so many interesting things to do, and I want to do them all. My faculty of Judgment keeps working for me, so I don't try to do them all at once.

UNDERSTANDING

There are two kinds of Understanding: Intellectual and Spiritual. Intellectual Understanding is realized after the collection of information from different sources outside of ourselves, including our history and conditioning. It can change from moment to moment. And the conclusion we draw may or may not be accurate.

With Spiritual Understanding, there is no question of inaccuracy. Our Understanding is whole and complete. It is the invisible movement of Spirit within us. Many times we can Understand something intuitively, but not intellectually. I think that intuitive understanding—KNOWING WITHOUT KNOWING—is Wisdom!

In Christian Healing (p.110), Charles Fillmore wrote:

> *To strengthen the will, and at the same time to discipline it along right lines, requires an understanding nothing less than divine. But we can balance our will and our understanding; when we do this we will always do the right thing at the right time. Nearly*

every mistake is the result of will's acting without the cooperation of its brother/ sister, understanding.

Understanding and Will must go together. Understanding is our ability to know that God stands under all things.

> Everyone then who hears these words of mine and acts on them will be like a wise man who built his house on rock. The rain fell, the floods came, and the winds blew and beat on that house, but it did not fall, because it had been founded on rock. And everyone who hears these words of mine and does not act on them will be like a foolish man who build his house on sand. The rain fell, and the floods came, and the winds blew and beat against that house, and it fell—and great was its fall!
>
> (Matthew 7:24-29)

In his sermon, Jesus is telling his listeners to not only hear his words and his counsel, but to act on them as well. In order to truly understand who we are and what it is we are doing in this world, in this incarnation, making peace with our past is necessary. My wife Sonya calls this *remedial healing.* Dr. Harold Bloomfield, a Yale-trained psychiatrist and author of seventeen books, believes, in *Making Peace With Your Past*, that the principal weight that keeps us stuck is *shame.* We are so ashamed of being ashamed that we try to suppress it, but it shows up when we don't feel good enough, or smart enough, or wealthy enough, or whatever. There is childhood shame from being treated horribly or adversely. In adolescence we are often ashamed of our bodies, or of not fitting in. The many perils of puberty leave us vulnerable to shame and the legacy of shame continues. This kind of shame is the feeling that "there is something inherently wrong with me," and many of the "D" words show up. We can feel defeated, deprived, defective, divided, deficient, despicable, disgraceful, deserted, diminished, debased, defensive, desperate, and devastated. The "D" words are the feelings left by shame.

There are some important questions we can ask ourselves to help jog our childhood memories that could be limiting us in our lives.

Did anyone abandon you? Were you neglected? Were you abused physically? Verbally? Sexually? Made to feel unwanted? Unacceptable? Useless? Were you compared unfavorably to other siblings or other children?

At the root of shame are some of the "psychic promises" that we inadvertently made, for example, *I'll become a replica of my parents; if I am just like them, they will treat me better.* We then adopt our parents' or caregivers' attitudes and behavior. Or we decide to rebel against their *ways* and behave the opposite. Most of us adopt and rebel and get caught into a push-pull inner conflict, which creates stress, tension, and feelings of uncertainty. Usually when we begin to unravel the chains that seemed to bind us, the feelings are not very comfortable but absolutely necessary. Our emotions get worn on our sleeves. To some extent emotions are automatic responses, but many are triggered by our past experience; we need to take a greater responsibility for understanding and responding appropriately to them. We don't have to solve the problem on the level of the problem. We can bring it to a higher level when we reach understanding. Our spiritual practices of prayer, meditation, reflection, and contemplation allow us to reach understanding thereby introducing into our process a deeper peace than we have experienced heretofore. However, the peace comes after the work, after the release through understanding. We then transcend of the struggles of personal history.

Tapping into Spirit gives us a way of including everything by integrating our past, not pushing it away or burying it. Many of our world leaders are beginning to model this for us.

Nelson Mandela spent twenty-seven years of his life in Robben Island Prison, much of it in solitary confinement, and he intuited that if he were to go on feeling hatred for those who had imprisoned him, he would carry his prison with him. His inner path to freedom -- to understanding, he realized—was to forgive. But that did not extinguish his fierce will to end injustice and free his people and, indeed, all of the world's people from injustice. So our integrity depends upon integrating Spirit into our lives, rather than trying to escape from our pain into Spirit. Spiritual teachings often attempt to skip over anger, but that doesn't work. We need to find balance through the twelve powers. We need to integrate our spiritual selves with our emotional, intellectual, and physical selves. In reality these "selves" can't be separated, only ignored. This process of integration helps us understand all the parts that make us whole. We learn to live more authentically with less suffering and more understanding.

Part of the *work* we are here to do is to discover and get to know who we really are. Who is really under the mask that we have been conditioned to wear? (Life review is part of our discovery.) True mastery requires us to break up the illusions of our life and live in reality. Courage, commitment, and faith are needed to stay with the process, which is integral to understanding ourselves. And then, truly, truly, our houses will be built upon solid rock.

Earlier in my life, I "understood" that most of my problems were due to the way my parents raised me; therefore, they were to blame. As I got older my level of Understanding deepened, and I became more patient. I spent more time with my parents and learned their struggles with life. After my mother died, I spent time with my father. Those years were precious. My relationship with him became stronger, and the experience during the years before he died contributed to my greater understanding of the life cycle. As I look back upon the time before my mother died, I see how understanding my dad had been with her. He took care of her until the day she died. He would tell others, "No one knows whose time it is next," meaning that he would do all he could for her while he was able. I did not appreciate his devoting his life energy during my mother's aging process, but I now realize the love and understanding he had. After mom died, Dad was released and became more alive. He had spent a lifetime "pleasing" and attempting to keep everyone happy. Now he was released to explore what he wanted for himself. There was real joy in watching him blossom. In turn, I came to understand my own patterns of "pleasing" and care-giving. Watching my dad's life cycle has helped me make new choices that add to my life rather than stifle it, helping me to bring different attitudes to my children and grandchildren.

IMAGINATION

Mind is the master power! We use our imagination to communicate with our selves, with our bodies. We create pictures in our minds that deliver messages to our bodies. Imagine the newspaper headline of a young woman lopping off her husband's penis as he slept. Whether you have a penis or not, picturing what that would feel like seems to be universally unifying. As the image is "felt," a physical reaction often occurs. Our imagination powerfully affects us physically. If I were injured and wanted to recover, I could picture myself recovered. This would send a signal to my body to help accomplish the healing. A technique used in sports training is to get the athletes to imagine participating in their activities with perfection. They see, feel, smell, and hear every detail of the performance. This technique alone has improved the performances of many athletes and teams.

Every little thing originates in the imagination of the mind. Through the imagination, the formless takes form. It is the picture-making power of the mind, the silent photographer of the soul.

In Lewis Carroll's book, *Through the Looking Glass* (the sequel to *Alice in Wonderland*), Alice and the Red Queen have a conversation, and in essence, Alice tells the Queen that as a child she would believe in as many as six impossible things before breakfast. She tells the Queen that if you start believing the impossible before breakfast, by dinnertime they are not impossible.

When we act on any discomfort, including thinking something is impossible, then it soon becomes more comfortable, and the impossible becomes possible. I remember a time when I had a desire to share what I had learned and had gained from many teachers and my experience by writing a book. The idea was divine, yet I had doubts. I was not a writer, and who would want to read what I had to say anyway?

But the idea stayed with me and, on reflection, I realize it was Spirit pushing me to my discomfort.

I began to put my ideas on paper, sitting at the computer for a minimum of one hour each day. I disciplined myself with the powers of Will, Order, Faith and Imagination to do something uncomfortable.

A Bible passage in First Corinthians basically says that the Lord searches all, hears and understands all imaginations and all thoughts. Inside of us, our imagination is the eye of consciousness. It is the projector of our potential. It is the mind of God (Spirit). My book idea was a potential from God Mind.

Imagination is conception that gives form to unformed mental energy.

We create with thought and feeling (seeing and feeling in our mind's eye), and that is the way we become co-creators with God.

Albert Einstein said, "Imagination is more important than knowledge." He also said that we live in a sea of energy. Others in the field of quantum physics have shown that we live in a universe where everything exists at various rates of energy. Where our thoughts go, energy flows. If we hold thoughts in our minds, we may choose to act on them, thereby producing the actuality of the thought we held. We imagine and help to create our own lives. Remember again, *where our thoughts go, energy flows*. If we imagine lives of misery and deprivation, we tend to create that in our own lives. So, if we imagine lives of joy and abundance, we also tend to create that.

Plato has suggested that we need to be careful of the images we put into our minds. Current research indicates that viewing or listening to images of terror, violence and/or fright suppresses the immune system. "Continually and repeatedly exposing yourself to images and stories of loss and devastation can make you physically sick and weaken your immune system," says Christiane Northrup, M.D. (from *Health Wisdom for Women,* November, 2001). Author Napoleon Hill said, "What the mind can conceive and believe, it can achieve." The choice is always ours —whether we use our imagination for good or evil. For example, holding a grudge or nourishing a fantasy of retaliation for a real or an imagined hurt usually produces uncomfortable sensations in the body: a rise in blood pressure, a flush of anger. If we want to experience serenity, we need to change our minds. This can be achieved through our other powers such as Judgment (Wisdom), Love, Order, and/or Understanding.

Michelangelo took a piece of marble and carved out the statue of David. The artist was asked how such a glorious work of art could emerge from a chunk of marble, and he said, "*I just took away everything that was not David.*" A Unity aphorism states: *Thoughts held in mind, produce after their kind.* Most methods of goal-setting and achieving use a type of visualization: see it, claim it, picture it happening, feel it as strongly as if it were real in the present, and imagine yourself already having it. This kind of visualization is effective in health. We focus our thoughts and mental picturing power on "seeing" and feeling ourselves being strong, healthy, whole, and well. Many coaches and athletes improve their abilities by practicing seeing themselves at peak performance. They do "mental rehearsals."

If we should LET GO AND LET GOD, what we are then doing is letting go of our own negative thoughts and letting God instill positive ones in their place. This becomes an open-ended imagination. In *letting go and letting God,* we open ourselves to new images (open imaging) rather than holding on to our old familiar pictures. This method transcends what we know and *lets go* to new possibilities. In this way we don't try to judge the images as positive or negative. Remember: both light and shadow are necessary to have a picture. Rain and snow are as necessary as sunshine, night as day, sleep as wakefulness, and rest as work. Bad dreams may have as much to teach us as pleasant ones. Finally, when we open ourselves to Spirit-consciousness, we can experience our natural creativity.

Images can arise in our minds from a dream, a song, a book, an intuitive hunch or other forms of inspiration. The invitation is to honor rather than censor the input. Imagine the inspiration that came to the poet-psalmist who wrote the Twenty-Third Psalm:

The Lord is my shepherd;
I shall not want.
He makes me lie down in green pastures;
He leads me beside still waters,
He restores my soul.

The good news about this form of imaging, *open imaging,* is that the Higher Power, the Higher Good, can come through our openness to the images.

During my days in Navy boot camp, we had been on a marching drill when we passed the base football team practicing before the season. Since I had played high school and junior college football, I imagined what it would be like to play for the Navy. The image of those days stuck in my mind, and I couldn't shake them from my thoughts. I kept imagining how wonderful it would be to play on the squad. This would be great duty, and the recognition would feel good. I saw myself in the lineup. I made arrangements to meet and talk to the coach. He discouraged me because they had college as well as professional players on the team, and I was relatively small compared to the others. I asked if I could try out anyway. He agreed. I kept the image alive in my head; when I completed the tryout, I was welcomed to the team. I had two successful years before being discharged from the Navy. I believe my calling into use the faculty of Imagination was what helped me.

ELIMINATION (RELEASE)

The last of the six thinking powers is Elimination (Release).

Release is letting go, or casting off, or changing our minds. We have the power to accept or reject. We can say yes or no. Either word is a complete sentence. Elimination can be the expression of our truth, no matter what. And in a true sense it is Surrender to Spirit—our truth is Spirit-centered. So elimination is not hanging on. It is allowing the truth of our inner spirit to manifest.

Each of us is evolving on the outer. But more important is the inner change that demands integrity and the full action of Spirit. And that means that our outer expression must align with our inner Truth that is Spirit-centered.

Release or elimination is our ability in the moment, to say NO to some situation, thought or emotion inside of us. For me, it was saying NO to my fear of writing and all those limiting thoughts. I kept myself going. And in the end there was no publisher to be found. I was dejected after receiving so many rejection letters, and a great deal of self-doubt was present. Yet, my truth was that I had something valuable to share. I slowed down but never gave up my vision. I kept eliminating the negative thoughts that emerged. My first book, Going Public, of course, was finally published. Now it has been translated into Spanish and Chinese and is being distributed to all countries where those languages are spoken.

When we are honest with our expression and inner thoughts, we are affirming who we are. Anything that we have told ourselves that keeps us from manifesting the full twelve powers can and probably should be part of our spiritual work. Spirit kept shoving me, and I listened and used every one of the twelve powers to keep on track. One never knows. Our task is to listen – to keep doing what is ours to do, and Spirit takes care of the rest.

It's been said that you can bury a stick, a tin can, or a bone, but you can't bury a worm. A worm will find its way and crawl out. I raise worms for recycling our garbage into fertilizer. I have several trays with holes in the bottom, and when the lower tray is filled, I place an empty tray on top with garbage in it. It's amazing to me that those little guys crawl up through the holes, and soon the upper tray is filled with worms eating garbage. They find their way out of the lower tray.

It's the same with feelings! Feelings have to be expressed. If they don't come out, the energy gets stuck and causes all kinds of physical, emotional, and psychological difficulties.

My journey at this stage of life is to release those ideas I grew up with of what being a successful person means. My father's voice (in my head) telling me to "learn the value of a dollar" still has the power to give me angst when I am not earning money. I do know the value of a dollar, and I learned that lesson well. But my interest these days is "serving" and sharing my gifts. My ideas of success do not match my early conditioning. I am making my life up now, and it is about giving and sharing. But staying in bed until 10:00 am and then going for a bicycle ride can be just as successful. We can create for ourselves what the meaning of success is. I am releasing old patterns as I become more aware of the ones that do not work in my life.

The following "things to do" are affirmations/meditations. The purpose of these affirmations for the Thinking/ Mental Powers is to fully integrate these faculties into your consciousness. You may want to read these words into a tape recorder, then listen to the tape. Saying or listening to the affirmation once will be insufficient to affect change. You will need to live with the affirmation in order to embody it. "Live with it" means to have the affirmation in your consciousness as you go through your day. You may want to take one affirmation per day (or week) and focus on it, making it your mantra.

What you can do:

Begin by relaxing your body using whatever technique is best for you. One idea is to sit where you're comfortable, then beginning with your feet, move up your body, one segment at a time, tightening that area then releasing. Next, observe the rise and fall of your breath and become quiet.

First thing to do

Now, focus your attention at a point slightly behind the center of your forehead and affirm:

Through the power of WILL within me, I am willing to do what is mine to do. I welcome change.

Journal what you discover doing this affirmation/ meditation.

Second thing to do

Move your attention gently down to the area behind your navel and affirm:

Through the power of ORDER within me, I listen to my inner voice and I am in the right place at the right time.

Again, journal your discoveries.

Third thing to do

Move your attention to the point just above and behind your navel, your solar plexus, and affirm:

Through the power of JUDGMENT within me, I make enlightened choices. I know when to say yes, and I know when to say no. (Journal.)

Fourth thing to do

Move your attention to the point in the center of your forehead and affirm:

Through the power of UNDERSTANDING, I know the source of my good, and I do those things that enhance my well-being. (Journal.)

Fifth thing to do

Move your attention to the point slightly in the back of your eyes and affirm:

Through the power of IMAGINATION within me, I form an image of the perfect elder I am becoming. (Journal.)

Sixth thing to do

Move your attention to the base of your spine and affirm:

Through the power of ELIMINATION within me, I release all thoughts, emotions, or actions that are not in alignment with my highest good. I let go and I let God. (Journal.)

THE SIX FEELING & SENSING POWERS:

Faith, Power, Strength, Zeal, Life, Love

FAITH

Faith is the perceiving power of the mind and is our insight, our ability to "see" our thoughts. Charles Fillmore, co-founder of the Unity Movement, defined faith as "*the perceiving power of the mind, linked with the ability to shape substance.*" Faith is our inner vision, our intuition to trust. It is our own computer software. Our brains are the hardware waiting to be programmed, and the key to successful programming is to employ Faith. Faith is our own inner light, our Spiritual essence. Faith is the ability to see ourselves as expressions of our *higher power* – God, if you will. This is the foundation and basis of our perception: the ability to see ourselves. Believing when there is no physical proof.

Faith can be developed if we are willing to trust our hunches, intuition, feelings, etc. "Faith is the assurance of things hoped for, the conviction of things not seen." (Hebrews 11:1)

The poet Rainer Maria Rilke writes, in *From Letters to A Young Poet*:

> ...that *everything* is gestation and then bringing forth. To let each impression and each germ of a feeling come to completion wholly in itself, in the dark, in the inexpressible, the unconscious, beyond the reach of one's own intelligence, and await with deep humility and patience the birth-hour of a new clarity: that alone is living the artist's life. Being an artist means

> not reckoning and counting, but ripening like the tree, which does not force its sap and stands confident in the storms of spring without the fear that after them may come no summer. It does come, but only to the patient who are there as though eternity lay before them, so unconcernedly still and wide. I learn it daily, learn it with pain for which I am grateful: *patience is everything!*

Faith was very challenging for me. I knew the words. I read books and heard teachers talk about the necessity of faith. But the reality of having it escaped me. I could say the words and even pray like I knew or trusted that by believing, whatever I wanted would manifest. I secretly thought that I was in charge of whatever happened to me. But the truth is that there is much we humans don't understand about the workings of Spirit. I learned to have faith through my intellect. Psychologist William James in his book, *Varieties of Religious Experiences*, explained that most people don't get spirituality as if struck by lightning or witnessing a burning bush, but through the "educational variety" because this awareness develops slowly over time. I thought that I needed to give myself permission to expand my experiential vocabulary. And the way I chose to do that was by taking a variety of risks to expand areas of comfort. The things I did were scary at the time but they were what I thought I needed to do. Probably the biggest risk I took was when I left a well-established profession in teaching for an uncertain future as a real estate broker. This was quite risky since I had a wife and three young children to support financially. I believed there was a certain way to live my life, and I had it all figured out. At the time I made the professional change I thought I was making a rational decision, but in retrospect I see that it was my faith that allowed me to make the transition. Faith was my willingness to follow the impulse to change, and by so doing, I began my embodiment of Faith.

POWER

The deep meaning of Power can be easy to miss. Many people think that Power is physical strength or that another person has Power over them; this conjures up negative or painful memories. Even though an injury done by another wasn't intentional, the memories can still hurt. We all know about the negative use of Power. History's tyrants are well known: Hitler, Stalin, Idi Amin, Pol Pot, Saddam Hussein, and Osama bin Laden are some names that come to mind. Humankind's misuse and abuse of Power has caused great suffering. But, there is a positive use of Power that often goes unheralded.

Power is the ability to convert an idea into words that are spoken and the ability to then take action. An old Quaker saying advises, "Pray and move your feet." We have the power to take our ideas and move them into action. "Moving our feet" is the expression of the spiritual faculty of Power.

Many people do not recognize their gift of Power. Sometimes we give our Power away by imagining that others are more powerful. We blame others and avoid responsibility by saying things like, "You drove me to drink," or "You make me so angry," or "You're driving me crazy." What we are basically saying when we use these phrases is that some other (even a small child) is so powerful that we are powerless over ourselves. We become victims and "martyrs." We also give our Power away when we believe that others control our happiness: "You make me feel so loved," "Without you I have no meaning," or "I need your love to survive," etc. When we use these phrases, we not only disavow any knowledge of our own Power, we give up responsibility for our own happiness to anyone who will take it. We then expect another to continually provide us with happiness – making "the other" the responsible party. In essence, we are saying that another has the power to make us feel a certain way. The truth is that this Power is within us and is an innate gift from Spirit, so we may create the life we want.

Part of the faculty of Power is the power to rationalize. We are incredibly intelligent, and we can rationalize anything we don't want to look at within ourselves. But we can't become content and truly full of joy until we are truthful with ourselves.

The greatest power we have is to understand and control ourselves. We need to look *under* what is motivating us. From what experience or person did this or that attitude arise? Was it from our culture, our caregivers, or some past experience? We need to be willing to look at our egocentricities.

The Buddha taught that the cause of suffering was egocentric desire. And the overcoming of suffering is not only recognizing this but dissolving it. We can use Power to recognize what isn't working for us and to let it go. "He who finds his life will lose it, and he who loses his life for my sake will find it" (Matthew 10:39). I interpret this as telling us to lose what isn't working and to use our power to change and do what works. We can let go of our egocentric ways and be honest with ourselves. We can move from the victim position to victory over our own personalities. We can "move our feet" by taking action.

Power is the ability to start and to complete things. Power creates spiritual dominion within us. There are many folks who feel helpless when faced with adversity. Power is our latent capacity for action from the inside to the outside.

We are agents and conduits for the Divine; therefore, there are no limits to our personal power. During a crisis, Power gives us opportunities to choose, to be negative about what is happening or to look for the "good" and discover what we can learn from it. The faculty of Power is that it gives us the strength to choose.

For me, the action came with the idea that I was not very musical. I was reared in a home that had no music. My parents had no musical interest and discouraged mine when I showed interest in learning a musical instrument. When I attempted to sing, others would cringe at my being off-key. I had no comprehension of what was wrong or even what being off-key meant. I grew into my mid-thirties with no understanding of music and no further interest in pursuing its study.

By the time I was about thirty-five, I recognized a desire to fill the lack of musical training in my life. I became interested in learning guitar and began taking lessons. My teacher thought I might be tone-deaf and sent me to a vocal coach to teach me to hear. My vocal teacher acknowledged my voice but surmised that my ear was untrained. From that beginning, I followed a course of studying with private teachers in both guitar and voice along with taking classes at the local community college. I began to express my Power through singing in the car, in the shower, to the wall, and on stage for amateur nights. I became more confident and self-assured as I communicated through the power of my voice. Now, I experience great pleasure when singing in groups, to my grandchildren, and whenever singing is called for. I discovered a whole new confidence and power through speaking, which came about by my challenging myself to risk doing something new. I have become acquainted with my own voice and am no longer intimidated by musical demands. In fact, I have become a proficient communicator through the Power of my voice.

In the workshops I do on GOING PUBLIC, we work with authentic expression that comes from the voice. The voice is an expression of Spirit. In most churches and synagogues, songs are sung. Singing is an important part of the worship service. We generally feel uplifted by song whether we listen or sing. We feel good.

Singing is communication. When we listen to a song, our emotions are often touched by the voice of the vocalist; when we sing and pay attention to the words—again, our emotions are often affected. That is because the voice is an expression of Spirit.

The voice is a power tool of communication. The idea is transformed into words, and then action can be taken. The voice is related to the Word. So, every little word is an expression of Power.

Words can create a wonderful, happy, full life. Or, they can create a dull, anxiety-ridden, and worrisome life. So many times we say words in our self-talk or to others without realizing the consequences and the power of every little word.

The very first chapter of the Gospel of John begins with, "In the beginning was the Word, and the Word was with God." This means that God's word called all things into being, so all things are of God. This has deep metaphysical meaning, because the Word is one of the vital connections we have with Spirit.

Through our words both vocal and sub-vocal we call all things into Being, thus becoming co-creators with Spirit. Fillmore explains the word as the "mind seed" from which springs every condition. Great stress is laid on the power of the word, both in scripture and in metaphysical interpretation of the scriptures. The word is the most enduring thing in existence. That is a powerful statement.

Every little word is reflected in one's state of consciousness, so if we want to change or transform our consciousness we can do it by – you guessed it – changing the words we use, and since words are the most "enduring thing in existence," we are counseled to keep our word.

Yet, how many times do we not keep our word?

We don't begin by saying to ourselves, "I'm saying this but I don't mean it," or perhaps, "I won't follow up." Yet, anytime we don't do what we say we will do, whether for ourselves or for another, we are not keeping our word.

Telling the truth and keeping our word, no matter how trivial that may seem, is probably one of the most important things we can do. In doing so, we eventually discover that we have built self-respect and confidence, as well as having built our credibility with others.

How do you feel when someone tells you that they will do something for you, and then they don't do it? There are usually a variety of feelings – anger, disgust, disappointment, hurt, etc. But if a person does this to you more than once, you probably begin to distrust that person, don't you?

When my wife, Sonya, and I were in seminary we bought a used washer and dryer from an appliance rental company. The lint basket was chewed up, so the salesman said he would get a replacement for us within a few days. Several weeks went by with no replacement, so I called him. He said it was on its way—we should have it in a day or two. Several more weeks went by with no basket and no call from the salesperson. Again, I called him, and he apologized and said we would have it in a few more days. You might imagine that I was beginning to doubt this man's word.

Three more weeks went by and still nothing. I was angry, called again, and received many excuses and promises that it would be delivered in a few days. I wasn't holding my breath, but I gave him the benefit of doubt. Several more weeks passed, so I finally called the head office and spoke to the president of the company, who was apologetic and said he would follow up on the matter. The next day the part arrived.

The point is: When people don't keep their word we get upset or angry, don't we? And if it happens more than once, we learn not to trust or rely on that person for anything – period.

This was a minor experience, but I have had even lesser experiences such as people saying they would call or do something by a certain time and then not following through on their word. You have probably had similar experiences, either from family, business dealings, or a friend. You may have done it yourself.

I doubt that anyone does this intentionally. When we promise something, we *intend* to do it, but other distractions come up and we forget or think we will follow up later. It has been incidents like these that got me thinking of the importance and power of keeping my word—every little word. Each time I promise to do something and don't keep my word, a little of my integrity and power is lost, and my self-worth is threatened.

If we say to ourselves, for example, "I'm going to go on a diet" then eat a large portion of chocolate mousse cake or a triple scoop of ice cream with fudge sauce or something like that, our inner self begins learning to not trust what we say, and we usually feel confusion or conflict. We are not happy campers. People walk around in life mixed up. Not any of us, of course, but some folks out there!

Again from Charles Fillmore:

> Man has the power to deny and dissolve all disintegrating, discordant, and disease-forming words. Knowledge of this fact is the greatest discovery of all ages. No other revelation from God to man is to be compared with it. You can make yourself a new creature, and you can build the world about you to your highest ideals.

By speaking the truth and keeping our word – to ourselves and others – we have the power to lift our consciousness to new heights. It doesn't mean we can't ever change our minds once we say or promise something. But if we do change our minds, we need to remember to use common courtesy by letting the other person know what is happening. We can call and make a new agreement. It's when we ignore our commitment that damage is done – to the other person involved and to ourselves. It is through keeping our word that we build self- respect. It is through keeping our word that others learn to respect us.

When we have kept our word, we feel an inner strength that comes from the confidence that our action has built. When we keep our word we are in a very high state of spirituality, and we keep ourselves in the Divine flow of Good. So we need to remind each other that our word is our connection with God. When we lose sight of the importance of keeping our word through commitments, promises, and agreements – both to ourselves and to others – we betray that connection with God.

Nothing seems more exasperating than depending on someone who doesn't come through. When we keep our word, we become more believable and others learn to trust and respect us. More importantly, we learn trust in and respect for ourselves.

STRENGTH

Strength is the power that is essential to the whole process of awakening our spiritual faculties because, without strength, we do not have the stamina necessary to follow through and unfold the other powers. In the physical realm, strength is vitality, endurance, and the ability to resist. In the mental realm, strength is that quality of mind that enables us to lead, to accomplish, to follow through on decisions to establish our purpose in life, and to hold firm to spiritual principles in daily living. Strength expresses stability of character and is closely allied with faith. Faith must continually be strengthened.

Humans are the only entity on earth that can think in abstracts and thereby act upon that thinking. Since many of the choices we make don't always present us with "happy endings," we need to become more "conscious" (more aware) before we even choose. And the greatest thing we can do is to dedicate ourselves to the development of consciousness. We can never be too old to seek and find ways to expand our consciousness. Life review is one of the tools that can create more compassion and understanding of our life patterns. Many of us are willing to go to any lengths to numb and distract ourselves from feelings of pain — -emotional as well as physical. (The exercise called "Life Review" helps us confront those patterns. Please refer to the journal exercises at the end of chapter one.) Sometimes our focus is on the brokenness, and we don't notice that we have become stronger at the broken places. When bone fractures heal, they become stronger than the original bone. Nature teaches us a principle in the body that is also true in the soul.

Why is pain necessary? Jean Houston, anthropologist, psychologist, writer, observes that "Illness opens the doors to a reality, which is closed to a healthy point of view." Becoming stronger is not about finding easy solutions to every difficulty or cures for every illness. Real strength is when we discover we can face difficulties with grace and presence and reopen the study of healing by changing our focus. We may not only survive but also thrive by strengthening ourselves when we turn our attention from disease and death to health and life. Pain can be our teacher and protector.

The twelve wonderful gifts from Spirit, inherent within us, need to be brought into the realm of our awareness in order that we may develop spiritually in a balanced way. In understanding our gifts we may apply the correct tool for the correct resolution.

The twelve powers are a balancing process. Most spiritual traditions have such a process that is intended to balance body and mind. In mystical Judaism, the Kabbalah contains the "tree of life" which consists of ten attributes to balance and strengthen one's life.

To convey "chi" or power throughout every system in the body, much of Asia practices the healing system of acupuncture, a system that focuses on twelve major meridians or energy channels.

In Greek mythology and many ancient cultures, the twelve powers are often depicted as gods and goddesses, such as Athena, who represents wisdom and strength.

Many of the body therapies, like Rolfing, Alexander Technique, Pilates, Hatha yoga, Feldenkrais, Aston Patterning®, Continuum Movement, et al, focus on balance.

True strength is balance. A well-balanced person is truly strong. Balance can manifest as quietness, inner confidence, poise, ability to keep peace, non-resistance, the ability to refrain from retaliation, negotiation, returning good for evil, patience, tolerance, steadfastness, and forgiveness. The Hebrew Bible prophet Isaiah said *". . . in returning and rest you shall be saved; in quietness and in confidence shall be your strength."* (Isaiah 30:15). Simply by being silent, we can center ourselves – a place that ultimately allows us to hear that still, small voice within.

We often equate strength with power, force or money. But there is an inner strength that is quiet, calm, still. Finding the balance is the key. Step inside rather than outside. Phil Jackson, who has coached for the Chicago Bulls and the Los Angeles Lakers, meditates. He relates in his book, *Sacred*

Hoops, that players under his guidance—Michael Jordan and company – had silent practices that enabled them to get into the flow, the zone. In this same way, we can become more still, more awake, centered, and focused. We can find our strength in life.

When I was in high school, I was planning on going to college. I wasn't sure what I would major in, but I was planning to attend. A teacher told me to think of something else because I would never make it in college. I remember feeling terrible because I thought I wasn't good enough. I discussed it with my parents, and my dad didn't care if I continued in school. He was strongly influenced by the Great Depression and thought it best for me to learn a trade. He wanted me to learn his trade and become a locksmith while my mother wanted me to go to college and become a professional. The reality was that my parents did not have money to put me through college. I was caught in a push-pull conflict between my desires, those of my parents, my disapproving teacher's, and a perceived lack of money. I was forced to rely on my own desires and move forward with what I believed to be best for me. I found that a great deal of strength was necessary in order to persevere and go to college. I had reservations about going, thinking I was not good enough (my teacher's influence) and that I was going against what my dad wanted of me. As I reflect, I think I felt challenged to go after what I wanted. When I decided to accept that challenge, Strength allowed me to pursue my college education successfully.

ZEAL (Enthusiasm)

Zeal is the great universal impulse that is the impetus for action. Enthusiasm or zeal is the urge or impulse underlying all advancement. It is the essence of fire and zest for living. When zeal is present, we are commanded to go forward rather than stagnate. The power of zeal challenges that part of us that wants to be safe and comfortable and tied to the way things are. Zeal needs the balance of the other powers to keep it from running rampant, consuming our life energies in its single-minded pursuit of goals.

Zeal is the power to have intense faith and to shape substance, so we need the cooling effects of judgment (wisdom), of spiritual discrimination. Some of us hold a lid on zeal, resisting the impulses of excitement because of conditioning that taught us to "stuff" our enthusiasm. The message we may have received was to not get too excited, since it may not work out and disappointment will surely follow. However, zeal propels a continuous momentum for changing. We find life easier if we stop resisting the river and just go with the flow. Zeal helps us let go and not be so controlling of process and outcome. The best way to practice this is to be reminded that we have a power greater than ourselves that guides us, if we are willing to listen.

We are *process beings*, and when we stay aware to that fact, we recognize that we are designed to change – it is our very nature. By keeping this awareness, we don't need to hang onto old ways with a death grip or fear anything new.

An attorney I once knew questioned me about my own process of life change, and I was amazed that at the end of my soliloquy he told me that he didn't want to change; it might upset his life. I lost track of him, but I still wonder if he had been able to hang onto that philosophy for very long.

Life brings situations and circumstances that force change. We can either accept the process or resist; that is our choice. But we need to remember that resistance is painful. If you press both hands together in an isometric exercise, pressing one hand against the other as hard as possible, you will experience tension throughout your arms, and throughout your body, if you hold that pose. Drop one hand, and the resistance disappears.

In my experience as a Rolfer, I have found that many people have bodies full of tight contractions with resultant discomfort. As the body loosens under my hands and becomes more resilient, clients report a greater ease in not only their bodies, but in their lives as well. Just as each of the powers need each other for balancing, the body thrives on balance also. When there is ease in the body, there is ease in one's life.

We are a gestalt and not separated parts. Everything works together, and each part affects the other.

Zeal works for anyone who employs it. It may be necessary to engage wisdom and love in its use. Zeal can move you forward instead of keeping the status quo.

Zeal has been the grounding in all of the challenges and risks that I took on. It was my enthusiasm that gave me the energy (and provided the Strength) to tackle seemingly unreachable goals. Many times I would say yes to a challenge and gather my zeal as I learned and explored virgin areas. For me, zeal became the faculty that allowed me to abandon intellectual analysis, to plunge into the feeling of joy and excitement. My mind's nay-saying voices would often get in the way of my excitement for a new activity, but it was my zeal that provided the energy for me to move ahead and enjoy each activity I undertook.

Well into his nineties, only a few months before his death, Charles Fillmore wrote, "I fairly sizzle with zeal and enthusiasm and spring forth with a mighty faith to do the things that ought to be done by me."

LIFE

We choose to live, to rise out of limitation, lack and difficulty into greater life. We choose life! We are immortal Beings who are "sage-ing, not just age-ing," in the words of Rabbi Zalman Schachter-Salomi. We always have a choice of how we think about a situation or ourselves. Our lives are a series of choices. We are said to have 50,000 thoughts daily. That's a lot of opportunity for choice. In our lives, there are losses, disappointments, heartaches, break-ups, failures – things that just don't work out. People go their own ways, and changes occur that we didn't expect and are not ready to accept. This is simply a fact of life. But life is more than these miseries. We can choose not to focus energy on thinking of these events as negative, and turn to Life. We can have the will to live strongly. We can make conscious choices to rise up and start anew, to set new goals, to recover from loss, to love again, to build new lives, to have the wisdom and good judgment to see beyond what was to what *can* and *will* be.

Instead of simply adding years to our lives, we can start adding life to our years. We don't want to come to the end of our lives with the feeling that we haven't lived. We can use those moments of our lives that we have judged to be insignificant as tools to renew and re-energize ourselves. As we wait for the red light to change, as we stand in line at the supermarket, or while we wait at the doctor's office, we can take advantage of these moments to reflect, pray, relax, and find our centers of peace instead of distracting ourselves with resentful thinking, magazines, radio, or constantly looking at others who seem to be holding us back. These moments provide opportunities for energy boosts rather than drains.

The life I was living with my family during the late '60's and early '70's felt stifling. My life force was dragging, and I began to question my existence. The culture during that time was emphasizing the challenge of belief systems. I became involved with meditation and spiritual studies of mind expansion. Also, my new path led me to many body and mind therapies. I came to realize that my marital relationship was not supporting my new awareness. I had to make a change and, as painful as it was to leave my family, I chose Life and continue to choose Life. Looking back, I see my choice was absolutely appropriate and, although there are scars of growth, the end result is that everyone affected by my choice has developed. I have remarried and continue to have a strong relationship with my three children and former wife.

LOVE

Love is a spiritual power. Love is a constant part of our Being and is not only an emotional state that we fall "in" and "out" of. Most of us have heard it said "You have not really lived until you have loved." Often, this is interpreted as meaning one needs to find the great love of one's life. Fortunately, that's not what it means. Simply, it means that if we don't experience the joy and the fullness of loving others or "an" other, then we haven't enriched our lives. This "love" is a deep caring for a relative, a friend, or a pet, as well as the "love" that convinces us to marry someone.

To love is to be in the flow of life. But so many times we restrict our free and inherent flow of loving. From *Twelve Powers In You,* (pp. 30-31), is a metaphor for this restriction: imagine a rubber band around your finger as representing prejudices and grudges. As you keep wrapping the band around your finger, you feel it begin to tighten and restrict movement. Each wrap represents a negative attitude such as attitudes of being "holier than thou," a desire for revenge, or a feeling of being superior to others. When we restrict this inherent flow of loving, we are essentially winding the band around our circulation process. We cut ourselves off from the life flow and hurt ourselves in the process. Soon the finger starts to swell, and redden, and hurt. Then it could turn blue from lack of circulation. But if we let go of old prejudices, hatreds and negative hard feelings and, if we forgive, release, desire good to come to all, then as it is said, we let go and we let God. As you remove the rubber band, the flow begins taking place. There is a vital flow of fresh blood that nourishes and restores, reinvigorating the finger. The life force wants to be free to circulate and needs our cooperation by opening ourselves, freeing our restriction to become more loving, forgiving and accepting of ourselves and others. We need to give and receive in positive ways that allow us to thrive in the flow of a greater life.

God said, "Let us make humankind in our image, according to our likeness..." And what is this image? "God Is Love." (1 John 4:8)

Most folks think of Love as something that comes *to us* rather than as something we intrinsically *are*. The early Hebrew writings, and later Jesus' words, teach us to love our neighbors as we love ourselves. This, I think, means that we can't really love others unless and until we can love ourselves.

We can learn to love ourselves in healthy ways. We can learn to take and enjoy quality, relaxed time. We can change our habits of eating, drinking, smoking, exercising, and watching television so that we feel better about ourselves and acquire more positive self-images. We can discover what we need to do to become more supportive, forgiving, proud, hopeful, and trusting of ourselves. When we are willing to look at and take action in these areas, then we can truly love ourselves – truly respect ourselves in authentic ways. From this place of self-love and respect we find that we can truly serve others.

Love is a healing power. We can respect each other instead of *needing* or trying to manipulate another. We can listen to each other. We can practice reflective listening—listening without judgment. We can reach out to those who are different—those who have discriminated against us—those who need help regardless of who they are. We can begin to extend ourselves beyond our own selves to become a positive energy for good in the world. Remember, we can't give anything away. All we do comes back to us. When we give positive love, we can be assured that love will come back to us ten-fold.

Love has been the glue that held and continues to hold my life together. There was a time when I did not know what love was. No one ever properly taught me, and it was emotional/ sexual love that I thought was love. As I became more educated through reading spiritual books, participating in a variety of mind-expanding seminars and workshops, and learning to meditate, I began to experience a wider definition of love. My new personal concept of the meaning of love included not only the emotional quality but also incorporated a wider vocabulary of loving activities that fed my emotion — beginning with the thought that there was more to experiencing love than the emotional high one feels (especially in romantic love). For me, getting outside of myself by thinking of and helping others gave me a whole new sense of love. Serving in the community and serving others helped me understand love in deeper ways. Now, leaving places better than when I found them has become a spiritual practice of love. I discovered that my desire and willingness to learn has allowed my love to manifest in ways I never imagined. The simple act of holding a door open for another or paying the toll for the person behind me has given me as much pleasure as knowing that every person has the same love within them. My gift is to practice giving and allowing others to connect with their inherent loving. So much of what I do is simply giving others permission to do the same, if they so choose.

In his inaugural speech in 1994, Nelson Mandela quotes Marianne Williamson; this message epitomizes what I have learned from my own experiences:

Our deepest fear
is not that we are inadequate.
Our deepest fear
is that we are powerful beyond measure.
It is our light, not our darkness,
that most frightens us.
We ask ourselves,
“Who am I to be brilliant,
gorgeous, talented and fabulous?”
Actually, who are you not to be?
You are *a child of God.*
Your playing small
doesn’t serve the world.
There is nothing enlightened
about shrinking so that other people
won’t feel insecure around you.

We were born to make manifest

the glory of God that is within us.

It is not just in some of us:

it's in every*one.*

And as we let our own light shine,

we unconsciously give other people

permission to do the same.

As we are liberated from our own fears,

our presence automatically liberates others.

In review, the twelve spiritual gifts or powers are: Will, Order, Judgment, Understanding, Imagination, Elimination, Faith, Power, Strength, Zeal, Life, and Love.

What you can do:

First thing to do

Allow your attention to focus on the area in the center of your head and affirm:

Through the power of FAITH within me, I am free of worry and concern and can enjoy all that I do throughout the day. (Journal.)

Second thing to do

Move your attention to your throat area and affirm:

Through the power of POWER within me, I have dominion and authority over my thoughts. I speak my truth from my inner source of Power. (Journal.)

Third thing to do

Move your attention to the area of your lower back and affirm:

Through the power of STRENGTH within me, I am strong and capable. I am stable, steadfast, and balanced. (Journal.)

Fourth thing to do

Move your attention up to the back of your neck and affirm:

Through the power of ZEAL within me, I move forward with excitement, joy and enthusiasm. I fairly sizzle with zeal! (Journal.)

Fifth thing to do

Move your attention to the lower abdomen and affirm:

Through the power of LIFE within me, I am a loving steward of my creative and vital energies. I choose Life! (Journal.)

Sixth thing to do

Move your attention to your heart area and affirm:

Through the power of LOVE within me, I am loving and I am loved. (Journal.)

CHAPTER 12

THE WISDOM IN ACKNOWLEDGING OTHERS : THE MESSIAH IS ONE OF US

At a gathering some time ago, participants had contributed their talents and energy in performing (music or poetry), and the applause they received was perfunctory at best. Instead of thanking and acknowledging others for all the good we receive from them, I realized, we seem to take these acts for granted.

All the *warm fuzzies* we get from friends and family, all the care and support during those times we are in the dumps, the kindly word, the gesture, the thoughtful act – how often are these acknowledged? Thanking, acknowledging, and praising others is one of the highest forms of prayer that exists.

Prayer is our communion with Spirit, and when we acknowledge another in any form, it is a communion with

Spirit. There is an East Indian word used in greeting another, *namaste,* which means "the Divine in me greets the Divine in you." Imagine how different our world might be if all people approached each person with an attitude of *namaste.*

Many times I am in awe when observing those courageous people who risk themselves by sharing their song, their gift, their passion, a reading, their service or whatever, in any form; and when they are finished, they receive perhaps merely a polite hand-clap, when we could give an overwhelming acknowledgment with whistles and shouts. It is not the quality of the performance in our perception or judgment that is important. These people are sharing their authenticity, their nervousness, their risk, a part of themselves – and that is enough. Those who take the risk of sharing themselves deserve a hearty acknowledgment for their willingness to put themselves "out there" — putting their "butts on the line" for everyone to see, judge, and evaluate.

Many of us fear the scrutiny and will hold ourselves back from expression for that reason alone. It takes courage, for many, to stand up and be heard. We all need validation from outside ourselves.

Studies done with children have shown that when children get validation, they grow up with strong self-esteem. Many folks did not receive this validation in their youth because parents seem eager to give the message "Don't be better than me." We grow up not thinking very much of ourselves. Ideally, we should not need validation from the outside, but the truth is that we do. One of the ways self-esteem is built is to get acknowledgment from the outside.

It is important to me that I see and know the authentic selves of others. We can all do this by taking the time to look – to truly see (and listen to) – another. In some African tribes when a man sees another individual approaching, he will stand quite still, look intently at the other, raise his arm in greeting, and say, "I see you. Indeed, I see you." Be willing to take the time to see.

Many folks who are generous with their money, time, and energy, are chintzy about giving healthy, hearty acknowledgment to others.

I've looked at this phenomenon in myself. I've noticed that sometimes I feel angry or resentful of just ONE thing that Sonya has done, and I hold back telling her about it because I don't want to deal with what I think her response will be; that is when I generally hold back acknowledging her for all the other wonderful things she does, the wonderful person she is. As a result of acknowledging this behavior in myself, I'm inclined to think that when we hold back expressing our Truth to another, it then becomes difficult to express gratitude or acknowledgment to everyone. Holding back in one area keeps us held back in other areas.

We have barely begun to realize the power in acknowledgment. When we finally understand this power, we will not let an opportunity pass to give some form of praise.

Charles Fillmore, co-founder of the Unity Movement, wrote:

> Turn the power of praise upon whatever you want to increase. Give thanks that it is now fulfilling your ideal. The faithful law faithfully observed, will reward you. You can praise yourself and others from weakness to strength, from ignorance to intelligence, from poverty to affluence, from sickness to health.

That's pretty powerful encouragement for acknowledging and praising others. Imagine what it would feel like getting a phone call each morning telling you how wonderful you are—what a great person you are—how beautiful you are. Imagine your self-esteem beginning to blossom and swell with that kind of nourishment.

ACKNOWLEDGE EVERYTHING! When we lived in Tennessee we had outside lights in each of the corners of our house. The house was on a hill, so the light fixtures were very high and hard to reach. Well, one light burned out, and I am one who is fearful of heights. And that burned out light was mighty high. I kept procrastinating and finally got the courage to get our long adjustable ladder. Carefully and slowly I climbed each rung, got up there, and cautiously removed the bulb and replaced it while all the while being terrified.

I was so proud of doing that, yet I thought I should be able to do it in the belief that I'm a man and the job was mine to do. I secretly wanted to be acknowledged for doing such a scary thing, but I didn't want to ask for the acknowledgement. Seemingly, it was probably nothing for most folks, but for me it was BIG!

Sonya knows how I am with heights, so when I told her I fixed the light, she, in her infinite wisdom, praised and acknowledged me with fervor. I didn't like needing that acknowledgment, but it felt so good. The point I'm making is that we are invited to acknowledge everyone for everything.

We don't know what a person's "doing" means to that person. What seems insignificant to us may seem huge to the other person. They may act like they don't care, but they do. We can only imagine another person's challenge. We can't take the risk of missing an opportunity to give others a lift. We can avoid taking anyone or anything for granted. Let us become conscious of the wonders that others do and acknowledge them lavishly. It doesn't deplete our account and the dividends will be great. We are all on this earthly path together. We are invited to cherish and care for each other.

Respect

Find Spirit in someone, and you find Spirit in yourself, and vice versa. Honor what you have found in yourselves and others with praise and respect, and you will begin to see the dividends pour into your lives.

There is a story from folklore about a great monastery that has declined. The abbot decides to visit the rabbi in his hut in the woods to see if he might offer any advice that would save the monastery. Upon hearing the abbot's woes about the monastery, the rabbi only commiserates with him. When the abbot finally leaves, he once again asks the rabbi, "Isn't there anything you can say that might help me save this order?"

The rabbi responds, "No, I have no advice to give, except I can only tell you that the Messiah is one of you."

When he returns, the abbot tells the monks, "The rabbi said that the Messiah was one of us, and I don't know what he meant."

In the days, weeks, and months that follow, the old monks ponder the rabbi's statement and wonder if the words mean anything at all. They wonder if one of them could be the Messiah and if so, which one? They each think about the others – focusing on their hidden resentments – and why that one probably isn't the Messiah, but what if . . . ?

Then they began to treat each other with unusual respect. After all, one or the other of them might be the Messiah.

This monastery was located in a beautiful forest, and some folks came to visit the monastery and picnic there. The visitors sensed the extraordinary respect the monks had for each other. They found the monks attractive and compelling.

Later, the visitors who had first come began to return and bring friends, and friends brought their friends. In a few years, the monastery had once again become a thriving center of Light and Spirituality.

The human mind prefers everything comfy in a nice, neat package. Whenever situations or people make us uncomfortable and are not the way we expect them to be, we feel the agitation. And to justify our position of discomfort, we criticize, judge, or make excuses.

Yet in the story, it was each monk thinking that the other might be the Messiah that got them treating the others with respect and love. Imagine what our own lives might be like if, instead of seeing others as adversarial, we saw them as the Messiah?

I recall a story that Ram Dass shared years ago. More than thirty years earlier, he had left his teaching post at Harvard to pursue his spiritual journey. He had gone home for Thanksgiving, where his siblings and their spouses were making fun of him because of his recent treks to India and the new way of thinking he had brought home with him. They met him with much anger and resentment. At dinner he imagined they were sending visual daggers across the table at him.

Ram Dass very consciously sent hearts back at them. Daggers were flying at him, and hearts were being returned. He did this visually as well as in conversation. By the end of the evening, there was acceptance and love between all of them. His energy had changed their energy.

A master teacher, Jesus, was a process person. He didn't get instant enlightenment. He did his inner work. He spent years in preparation for his ministry. We must do the same and not run from the agitation or discomfort. We must avoid seeking refuge in familiarity – or comfort.

When I was Process Facilitator for the Association of Unity Churches, I sometimes went into churches that were in transition or in conflict, and what I usually found there is that folks get into cliques – for comfort – and many fail to honor and respect the others. In my experience, the main issues with churches that get in trouble are around communication.

We found the monks in the story were holding hidden negative thoughts about each other and not expressing them. Resentments can build in any relationship when the truth isn't told.

We hold back being truthful and authentic because of how we think the other person might respond to our truth. We have been taught to be *nice.* Spirit isn't necessarily *nice.* Always real, but not always nice! And in order for us to progress on this path of spirit, it is required that we tell the truth to each other no matter how uncomfortable the experience might be.

Yet, so many people are more interested in being *right* than in being honest. And many will fight tooth and nail for their power or status. In reality, telling the truth is honoring and respecting the divinity in each other and is the greatest gift of love you offer. Telling the truth allows Spirit to balance and heal any situation. When we recognize we all have the same spirit, we can embrace our differences.

What you can do:

First thing to do

For three days, look at those in your life who irritate you, who you find fault with or blame. List them (and your irritations) in your Journal.

Second thing to do

Imagine that these people are holy. Imagine how you would treat a holy person. Imagine the respect you would give that one. Journal your ideas.

Third thing to do

Put your ideas into action. Treat those on your list as though they were holy. Observe any changes (in yourself or in them) and include them in your Journal.

Fourth thing to do

Look for small ways to recognize and acknowledge others. Do it constantly. Then know how grateful you are for their being in your life. Include what others have done (in your life) in your Journal. Make acknowledging others a part of your philosophy. Thank others for thank-less acts.

Fifth thing to do

Choose three people in your life whom you appreciate and write each a letter telling them why. Include these letters in your Journal entries.

CHAPTER 13

THE WISDOM IN GIVING

As I grew older, I found my youthful eagerness to save the world had eroded and was replaced by hustle to earn "enough" money. Throughout this period, I was obsessed with making more and more money for my growing family. Seldom did I feel that I had earned enough, and the more I earned the more we spent. During those years, I could not see that *spending* time to make money came at the expense of other important life happenings (family, friends, Sabbath time). But as my energy and values shifted with age, I realized the importance of balance in my life. My attention moved to other interests as I let go of monetary pursuits.

I became more involved in community work. It has been delightful and very fulfilling to participate with others with no thought of financial gain – definitely contrary to all my early programming. I was learning a valuable lesson in the process—SERVICE. My suggestion is to balance life with earning and service. There is always a need in our communities for help with all kinds of organizations. Get involved – the benefits and the gift of serving will be paid back in dividends. Ultimately, you serve yourself by serving others.

Humans seem to be pulled toward helping others. It seems to be part of the human condition. The funny thing is that when we reach that level of *wanting* to help others, then our subsequent actions to that end bring us so much joy. That which we do for others we do for ourselves. We get "hooked" on this path of service; the more we serve, the freer we feel. The human desire to serve others seems to be inherent. There is a saying: Those who God wishes to bless, handily receive the means for helping others. What follows is an old Hasidic folk tale about Yussel the Miser.

Long ago, a homeless beggar came into town and found a cubbyhole where he could lay down his head. And he knew that the best place for a hand-out was in the better section of town. So he set out for this more affluent area, and eventually knocked on Yussel's door. He was invited to come inside, to enjoy some tea and cookies and conversation. Soon Yussel said to the beggar, "You knocked at the door for some purpose, what was it?"

The beggar replied, "Now that you ask, I could use a few rubles to get me through the Sabbath and the rest of the week."

Yussel became furious. "I invite you in for tea and cookies and we have such a wonderful time together, then you have the nerve to ask me for money. Get out!"

The beggar left Yussel's house and went to see the local rabbi to see if he could get a meal. The rabbi prayed and told him the areas to beg in and the areas to stay away from. Further, he told the beggar to stay away from Yussel's house because he was the town miser. "You will get nothing from Yussel!"

The beggar did what the rabbi told him, and he thought the rabbi's prayer had worked because on Friday morning he woke to find at the edge of his cubby hole an envelope with enough rubles for the Sabbath and for the rest of the week. Week after week, the beggar awoke to another wonderful envelope.

One day the rabbi heard that Yussel was ill and in the hospital, so he went to visit him. "Yussel," said the rabbi, "it would be good if you gave some *tzadaka* (some charity). It could help you now, and it wouldn't hurt when you go to the other side." Yussel just looked at him and said nothing. The rabbi left, and a few days later Yussel died. The miser's house was searched and, surprisingly, no money was found. In fact, nothing of enough value was found to even pay for Yussel's burial. So he was given a pauper's burial, no more.

That next Friday when the beggar awoke, he found no envelope. As quickly as he could, he went to the rabbi's, where he found lots of commotion as every beggar in town was there, complaining that they had received no envelope that morning. Soon they figured out that Yussel must have been delivering the envelopes. Everyone felt terrible and decided to scrape together whatever they could to give Yussel a proper burial.

At the gravesite, the rabbi was overcome and fainted, and while he was unconscious, he imagined he had a conversation with Yussel. The rabbi asked him, "So, how goes it?"

Yussel responded, "It's perfect here in heaven. Everything is taken care of. We have no needs. I feel so fulfilled! No, not really. I miss getting up at dawn every Friday and slipping the envelopes under the doors and in the cubbyholes. I have no chance to give here."

Here in this life is the only place we can give, feeling the joy and the benefit of giving.

As we age, we usually discover that we want to give back to the world. We awaken to our time for *conscious service.* We "chop wood and carry water" before our awakening, and we "chop wood and carry water" after. Work is the same, but the attitude has changed. The Sufis call those whose attitude is altered by enlightenment "the changed ones." All in all, those who reach this period consciously usually are happy people. Some get into service to community. Still others take time to be mentors and guides. The wise will share in the quiet. Observe these wise ones, and you will note that their special wisdom is revealed by a remark, a glance, or even the way they eat. With a moderate degree of effort, you, too, can be among these special people.

"More than a calf wants to suck, the cow wants to give milk."

The Talmud (Bible commentaries)

Our culture is moving very slowly in allowing our elders to give the "milk" of their wisdom to the younger generation and/or to their communities. However, to discover that wisdom we need to look at our history. According to Rabbi Schacter-Shalomi, the decade of our sixties is a time to recover our past. Wisdom comes from being conscious – consciously aware. And I think that if we consciously review our life experiences, we can draw wisdom and energy from them.

In other cultures there is a role for elders; they are held in high esteem.

They are the wisdom holders. They serve on counsels and have a place in elder circles.

Becoming an elder, however, doesn't automatically confer wisdom upon the one who is aging. Yes, we gain some wisdom by the mere fact we have lived, but consciously preparing ourselves for our elder years is what contributes to our wisdom.

Writing-journaling-seems to aid us in our insights. The process of writing crystallizes the thoughts. Journaling is where I discover a lot – about my feelings, beliefs and desires. Besides meditation, it's one of my most important contacts with Spirit. If this tool is not already part of your process, try spending five minutes or more per day recording awareness's of your aging process – how this process relates to family, friends, and others you share life with—both now and in the past. Be sure to include happy and positive events as well as the dismal and negative.

When we write our feelings and thoughts, we develop clarity on how we want to live the rest of our lives without regrets. This action really helps to prepare us for living lives of integrity, loving, and service. It's a way of becoming more aware of what we have to offer and what we can pass on.

Remember that Moses guided the people *to* The Promised Land but did not take them in. That's an inside job. And perhaps the Bible lesson for us is to guide others to their Promised Land. But we need to prepare to do that.

Love in Action

As we examine ourselves and look at our motivations for generosity or unselfishness, etc., we may find that they are self-serving means for making ourselves look good in the eyes of others. We may want to be seen as Mother Teresa or Mohandas Gandhi, but the nun and the Mahatma didn't give generously of themselves so that others would like them or revere them. They absolutely WANTED to do the things they did. It is no accident that we repeat throughout the ages such an axiom as, "Virtue is its own Reward." That sounded senseless to us when we were young. We could hardly conceive of something virtuous as being rewarding in and of itself. As we grew older, we discovered we were capable of selfless, generous acts that gave us much pleasure in the doing. When our thoughts intruded and suggested we be viewed as wonderful creatures for doing the things we did, we lost that original "reward." So, we need to be brutal in our honesty with self as we explore the depths. The authentic honesty to self will pay dividends in creating our fullness. Know Thyself! And to thy known self, be true.

Giving our time and energies to helping others actually brings us closer to the discovery of who we really are. The outcome from our serving others is less important than the process and the commitment.

What most of us want most is to have a feeling that we matter. Our fear is not of dying, but that we have not lived a full life, or perhaps that our lives have not made an impact on one or more persons.

Exploring the question of what "living fully" means, I reflect on the importance of Generosity of Spirit. Since I sometimes go to the Bible to get deeper understandings, I found in Romans 12:6-10, the message that essentially each of us has something to offer: we can give our time, treasure or talent, or all three.

One of the paradoxes of life is that the more we give up in money, time, or energy, the more we seem to have. I don't know how or why it works that way, but I know it does.

Service brings meaning and fulfillment to our lives in a way that wealth, power, possessions and self-centered pursuits can never match. From Luke 6:38: "...give, and it will be given to you; good measure, pressed down, shaken together, running over, will be put into your lap. For the measure you give will be the measure you get back."

In my own life I was really conditioned to take care of myself, and my perception was that others always wanted something from me. I learned to protect myself. I avoided volunteering for anything that wasn't self-serving. My life became very insulated. I didn't know that at the time, but in retrospect I see what I did to myself. I had read all the sayings and books and heard all the clichés saying it is better to give than to receive. I also went through the motions of giving when I was involved with many spiritual groups, but that had no meaning. My actions were mechanical and did not come from a true belief in generosity. When I did something, I wanted to know how it would help me with fortune, fame or power.

However, in the process of giving, mechanical as that was, I experienced something interesting. When I did volunteer in Napa, California (as a Police Chaplain, the County Commission on Self Esteem, and creating workshops in leadership activities for the community), I felt good. My giving fulfilled me. This surprised me because the message I received at a very early age was that "everyone is out to take advantage of you." I had learned to be on my guard.

When I was in my thirties, something began to shift in me, and I truly grasped the truth at which I had arrived: you can't give anything away; whatever you give comes back in a greater degree. What we have to give is our legacy.

In order to live a conscious life, we need to have an intention to be conscious. Conscious service is actually a gift to us. The path of Service is a noble one that benefits everyone. Each of us has gifts to share – from a particular talent, to life experience, to simply sharing our presence. Service is a double-sided coin that we can use on our spiritual path. One side of the coin of service is the manifestation of Love, and the other side of service is the outgrowth of Love. What we do consciously helps everyone and everything.

Sometimes, helping just happens, and caring is a reflex because humans have an innate generosity. Right attitude regarding generosity needs development.

Service or generosity is a major teaching in every spiritual and religious discipline. Our challenge is to develop the *kavannah* (intention) so that we are giving consciously. And again, in every tradition, whether a *Sanga*, a *Havarrah*, a church, any congregation where people gather with other like-minded folks is a special way to grow spiritually. There is something one learns only with sharing in a group, kind of like the "hundredth monkey" phenomenon, often referred to currently as "critical mass."

An old saying comes to mind: "Expect a miracle every day, but don't be surprised if you find only three or four a week."

A miracle of giving and receiving occurred in my life when one of my daughters inadvertently awakened me. I had been accustomed to her telephoning me to tell me her "life stuff" (you know: complaints about kids, husband, work) – just venting to someone who would listen. And I did—just listen. After all, as a minister, I am trained to listen, and I do it well. After some years of this relationship, I began to be aware that my daughter seldom "returned the favor." She didn't ask about my life or my wife's, whether we were having any problems, or if everything was okay. This became a growing resentment, and one day I admitted this to my daughter when she phoned. Her response to MY complaint was succinct: "But, Dad, you don't call me with your 'life stuff!' I listen to my friends when they want to vent because that's what friends do. But you don't call me to vent." Oops. This was a needed twist for my perspective. I got to look at this "problem" from another side and saw my own part in it. Ah hah.

Most of us are taught when we are young that "it is more blessed to give than to receive." I was practicing this with my gift of listening when my daughter called. Unfortunately, I forgot that I received something when I gave this gift. As with all giving, the donor gets something less concrete, but very real nonetheless. I felt good. I liked myself when I was giving to others. It's easy to get caught up in that mode and assume that's what your role is. The truth is, life is give and take. We can't all give if no one is there to receive. When my daughter reminded me that I don't call her to vent, I realized that I had denied her the opportunity to feel good about listening to my problems. It really does "work both ways."

What you can do:

First thing to do

Seek to become someone's friend rather than looking for someone to befriend you. Find a way to help someone in need rather than looking for meaning in your own life. This is simply a matter of how we focus on life. Journal the results of this exercise.

Second thing to do

Select three of your acquaintances or friends that you have little contact with, and call them. Tell them you were thinking of them, and let the conversation develop from there. Journal your results and what it felt like to reach out to another.

Third thing to do

When you are feeling lonely or troubled, phone a friend or acquaintance and dare to reveal this part of yourself. You are giving the gift of trust even while you receive whatever that person has to offer. Journal your process and your feelings about what took place. It's a good idea to note in your journal what resistance in yourself you encountered to do this exercise.

Fourth thing to do

You may have financial concerns, worries over money. If you are crossing a toll bridge, pay not only your toll, but the person's behind you. Be creative. Find other ways to give, such as paying for someone's meal when they don't even know you're there. This kind of anonymous giving pulls trust back into your life, trust that you will be okay. This is giving to give, not giving to get. Develop this consciousness of giving. Strangely enough, you can't really give anything away because everything ultimately comes back to you. What happens with conscious giving is that you open up opportunities (grace) to receive more than you give. With this new consciousness, journal your results.

Fifth thing to do

Make and bring a hot meal to a sick friend or a dessert to a neighbor. Check in with your community volunteer center and ask how you can help. (It's okay to direct your giving to areas that you are passionate about.) Note how you feel when you give to give, not give to get. Journal about this entire process.

CHAPTER 14

THE ENDING IS THE BEGINNING

T. S. Eliot writes: "What we call beginning is often the end. And to make an end is to make a beginning. The end is where we start from."

Basically, life seems to be a series of beginnings and endings. But there is more in between. The time between the beginning and ending is what the Bible calls the wilderness. I call it the tension of what's next. We probably live in that wilderness area most of the time and our challenge here is to learn how to live with that tension.

We are most uneasy during a transition, when some level of comfort is gone and we find ourselves wanting that new level of comfort to be here NOW. The wilderness is a time of exploring, learning what is needed, trial and error, falling down and getting up again. It is often a time of discomfort, yet it is always a meaningful time. Usually the old order is disrupted or disturbed. In a way I think we are always in the wilderness, but at different stages. In our personal lives it can be a time when our sense of what is real is challenged.

We tend to think of a new beginning in terms of an external change. But New Beginning actually is an internal experience. This was the case for Sonya and me when we took positions as ministers at the Unity Church in Knoxville, Tennessee. The church there had been without a minister for two years before we came along. The congregation was overstressed and tired; however, they had done a fine job of keeping it together without any minister. They were in the wilderness. When we arrived, there was such relief that someone else was in charge that they gave up all their prior efforts. And we, just getting started in ministry at that time, were naive and took it all on in our eagerness. (A sure ticket for burn-out.)

The most important factor in *keeping things together* is honest communication. That means to keep telling your truth. New beginning generally calls forth the need for new commitments, not always an easy task. Any commitment challenges us to take concrete action, to "walk our talk." Often discipline and sacrifice are required. A true commitment is not an obligation to something or someone outside of yourself, rather it is a commitment to yourself. It is an agreement with yourself to give up some freedom in a certain area of your life in order to enrich other areas of your life.

To be committed is to accept responsibility for being a creator in one's life. It means being willing to be the cause rather than a reaction to the circumstances. Remember the Zen saying: Before enlightenment, all day, chop wood, carry water. After enlightenment, all day, chop wood and carry water.

Commitment and cooperation were still needed back at that church in Tennessee. We needed them to continue what they had learned during their two years of wilderness. Moses led his people into the wilderness. They left Egypt and experienced forty years in the wilderness. And Joshua took them into the Promised Land. He could not have taken them into the Promised Land without their having had the wilderness experience.

A fragment of a poem by Dorothy Pierson, a retired Unity minister, seems to summarize the preceding: "God of all the days complete, Help me to understand The beginnings and the ends. And, in so doing, Go renewed and free into the new day you plan for me." And from the book *Illusions*, by Richard Bach: "What the caterpillar calls the end of the world, the master calls a butterfly."

We live continually with beginnings, middles (wilderness, tensions) and endings. Perhaps they are all the same. The challenge is to learn to live that middle tension with some degree of comfort. We can do that if we learn to appreciate the wilderness. Knowing that this pattern of beginnings, wilderness, and endings is simply how it is on this planet can help us cope and appreciate the challenges as they arise.

One of these challenges is to acknowledge that we will not live forever, and certainly others will survive us. As we are creators in our lives and committed to ourselves, so must we accept responsibility for those who come after (or those who will clean up after). So we don't leave messes for others to deal with after we have gone, we commit ourselves to becoming practical elders.

In this regard, Appendices II & III give concrete actions to ensure a smooth transition from this life to what follows, while Appendix I contains information that can help you maintain or improve your health as you age.

Finally, whether or not you have done the activities at the end of each chapter or used the information in the appendices, by reading this book you have come a long way in *wising up* to become a wise elder.

What you can do:

First thing to do

From Chapter 3, read and add to, if necessary, your "Autobiography," "My Ideal Elder," and "Who I Chose To Be. "

Second thing to do

Read aloud, "My Ideal Elder" and "Who I Choose To Be" once a day for 21 days. Then, don't read for 7 days; then read another 21 days with 7 days off, then again for 21 days.

It may seem tedious, but do it anyway. By reading it aloud, you integrate the ideas into your subconscious and you are doing your part in creating change. The experience of doing this exercise can change life patterns that are limiting. The mystery and the magic happen just by doing the "work."

APPENDIX I: HOW TO CARE FOR YOUR HUMAN SELF

Use it or Lose it

Everyone benefits from exercise and play. As we age, we lose muscle mass: a program of muscle conditioning and strengthening is helpful and healthful. Movement is also important. Perhaps we can't be as aggressive with physical movement, but moving is essential to maintain health.

As we've begun to age, we gradually notice that we have less flexibility, that there may even be stiffness in various joints. This is not a sign from above to settle more deeply into the recliner. We do not need to become more sedentary. If our bodies are able to move at all, then we must be diligent in moving them. When we stop moving, we regress. Contrary to popular belief, it doesn't take a great deal of exercise to remain fit. A half-hour brisk walk three to four times per week works. If it is difficult to walk fast, then do what you are able, but move. It's best to get the heart rate up, so go to your own edge of tolerance and increase your heart rate as you are able.

Physio-balls are large "beach-balls" made especially for weight-bearing – for people to sit or roll on. These balls are used for muscular conditioning, strengthening, balancing, coordination, and physical therapy, and are gaining in popularity since they are excellent for doing a variety of movements and exercise. You do not have to belong to a gym to use these, although in the beginning it would be good to get some guidance for your specific structure. Focus and intention are imperative as you perform each movement. Learning your particular patterns of movement will assist you in correcting any structural deviations that may be causing you pain or stress.

The body is meant to be alive, active, and healthy. It knows how to heal itself if given the chance. However, past physical traumas, accidents, and conditioned patterns of misaligned movement hinder the body's ability to heal. If we can become aware of misalignment and patterns of abnormal movement brought about through accidents or mimicking our parents or other caregivers, then we can correct ourselves through conscious movement.

Some of the most beneficial and least damaging forms of exercise include Pilates, Physio-ball, yoga, Tai Chi, weight training, and Continuum Movement. Biking and walking can be done at any time or place. Swimming and water aerobics are excellent exercises if walking is painful or puts too much stress on joints as the water bears the body weight.

The following are several systems to consider:

Continuum Movement, a method of outer movement emulating the body's natural inner rhythms, is designed to free us from our conditioned "holding" or tension patterns, thereby allowing healing to take place.

Pilates, a system originally developed for bed-ridden hospital patients, focuses on the inner strength of the body, the core structure, and incorporates the use of floor mats and/or an apparatus of springs known as a reformer.

Hatha Yoga, a form of yoga, is a collection of postures that focus on specific areas of the body encouraging strength, lengthening of muscles, flexibility, etc.

The slow-moving postures of Tai Chi have been practiced for centuries in China. Its objectives include calmness of mind, improved balance, flexibility, muscle strength, and improved immune system.

Alexander Technique is a method of movement education designed to encourage more efficient movement of the body by the use of appropriate body alignment and posturing.

Feldenkrais® is a system designed to increase mobility and range of motion through education and body/muscle manipulation.

Aston Patterning, Rolfing, Structural Integration, and Heller Work are systems that focus on movement efficiency through body movement education and soft tissue manipulation.

If no *physical* movement is possible or there is limited physical movement, benefits still may be obtained through conscious conditioning with a competent instructor from the above methods.

Have Fun

The above systems are mentioned as suggestions to keep your body in optimum health. The best part, of course, is just having fun. You won't be paying much attention to your heart rate if you're out on the tennis court with your best friend and dashing from one side to the other to return the ball. You're just having fun, and your body is getting the benefit from it. Not just your body is benefiting. Your outlook on life, your attitude and perspective are also becoming healthier. Whatever physical endeavor you choose to keep yourself in optimum health, remember to have fun.

Are You What You Eat?

So much is written about diet and its effects on body health. Every diet book author professes that his or hers is *the* ONE. After exploring every diet and fad that came along over the years, I finally woke up. I am my own best teacher about what foods to eat. As individuals, we are unique. Our histories are unique. Our body's physiology and individual chemistry are special. What is one person's health food is another's poison. My wife is able to eat a high protein diet and thrives. If she eats too many grains, she gains weight and is hungry and depressed. I, on the other hand, thrive on grains. If I limit my diet to proteins and fatty foods, I feel terrible and am starved. Nevertheless, diet promotion pushes for the same foods for everyone. I don't think so. Be your own nutritionist. Trust your feelings and intuition. Since childhood we are taught that everyone else knows more than we do. Many health practitioners promote this, so we become adults not trusting ourselves. You may thrive on animal protein like my wife. Check this out for yourself. Quite frankly, I eat a little of everything. I don't avoid red meat, but I limit it in my diet. My diet consists of mostly grains, vegetables, and fruit; occasionally I even have chocolate and ice cream. Too much emphasis on any one thing dries up the juices of life. Let us allow our good sense and reactive feelings to guide what we eat and the quantity of our food and drink.

What you can do:

First thing to do

In your journal, write down ten activities that you consider to be fun. Notice, while you are writing them down, what makes these activities fun for you. During the next week, do two or more of them. Return to your journal and record what it felt like to have fun. (There may be a common thread between the activities you have chosen that nourish you and inspire you to continue to treat yourself. The child part of yourself will always need to be expressed. Ignoring this important aspect of play in your life can create imbalance, leave you feeling depressed and unfulfilled.)

Second thing to do

When we walk, some of us lean backwards as we move forward – the unconscious message in this method is that we are holding back while forcing ourselves to move forward. Some others of us hold ourselves absolutely vertical and use extra muscles by making ourselves walk rather than allowing gravity and momentum to do the job. The most efficient method of walking is to be leaning from the ankles slightly forward into gravity, allowing ourselves to move with a sense of forwardness. When our entire body participates in this posture, gravity pulls us forward with ease. The unconscious message we give ourselves is that we are one hundred percent in harmony with the direction in which we move, it is then that the motion is effortless. When all parts of us are working together, we become truly centered. As Chuang-Tse said, "When the ten thousand things become one, then we return to the center, where we have always been."

When we become more aware that the space between A and B, our beginning and ending, is more important than these two points, then we have begun the conscious process: the journey.

Third thing to do

Explore one or more of the body systems outlined in this chapter or others in your community to experience your body in a new way. Consider investing in a private trainer for six to ten sessions in a system that you feel drawn to.

Fourth thing to do

Keep a food diary for three to five days, noticing your energy levels and other effects associated with the foods you eat. Consider counseling with a nutritionist.

APPENDIX II: NOTEBOOK FOR SURVIVORS

Create a notebook for yourselves and those who will survive you. It is beneficial and an act of love to not leave those behind you with a mess to figure out. The notebook should provide information on where your *will* may be found, location of insurance papers and your investments, your bank accounts, location of keys and other important data. All of us will definitely "get old," but old age doesn't automatically confer wisdom. If we want to "Wise Up," then we need not only to take responsibility for choices in our lives, but for what will happen to those around us after we die.

The following is adapted and modified from the Beneficiary Book (a computer program with appropriate forms can be ordered — see resource section).

Here are questions that you may want to answer and include in your notebook FOR BOTH YOURSELF AND PARTNER/SPOUSE:

YOURSELF:

Your birth date, place of birth, Social Security Number, driver's license number. Parents' names and their places of birth.

Name, address and phone number of employer.

Address and phone number of former spouse(s) and date(s) of divorce.

Do you have: will, trust, birth certificate, prenuptial agreement? Where are they kept? If you don't have a will, consider getting appropriate counsel.

Do you belong to any organizations that might entitle your family to benefits? Veteran benefits?

SPOUSE/PARTNER:

Answer the same questions as above

CHILDREN & GRANDCHILDREN:

Names, addresses, phone numbers, social security numbers, sex, and birthplace of each child and grandchild.

MEDICAL HISTORY INFORMATION

Blood type, Location of living will or durable power of attorney, names, address, and phone number of health care provider and/or personal doctors, name(s) of your medical insurance company and policy number. What medical problems have you had either in the past or present, dates, treatment? Medications you take.

FAMILY MEDICAL HISTORY

Names of each immediate relative, date of birth and/or death, cause of demise along with any medical facts i.e. high blood pressure or diabetes etc.

ADVISORS

Names, addresses, phone of your lawyer, stockbroker, accountant, banker, financial counselor, insurance broker, real-estate agent, and tax advisor(s).

FINAL ARRANGEMENTS

Give details of your wishes (include names, addresses, & phone numbers where appropriate) to the following:

Durable Power of Attorney, Names and phone numbers of who to call first, Name of person to handle funeral arrangements, Cemetery or cremation arrangements, Memorial service, memorial gifts, After funeral gathering, Budget for final expenses, Spiritual/cultural thoughts, Arrangements for passing on personal items (Including special bequests).

ESTATE

Give location, date of execution, name, addresses, phone numbers of attorneys involved for the following:

Will, Trust (exact name), Trustor(s), Trustees, Trust tax ID number, Guardians for minor children, Probation attorney.

LIFE & HEALTH INSURANCE

Names, addresses, phone numbers, agent(s) and companies. Include policy date-location-beneficiaries-premiums with due dates, Group or private health coverage.

RETIREMENT PLANS

Company: plan number-contact person, survivor benefits, beneficiaries, IRA/Keogh/Other—location of certificates along with Broker or Agent's names addresses and phone numbers.

BANKING

Names, addresses, phone numbers, account numbers, and contact persons of Banks, Investment institutions, Money owed to you (by whom, terms, and amount) and Financial obligations you owe (to whom, terms, and amount).

INVESTMENTS

Names of Securities, Stocks, Mutual funds, Real Estate, Bonds, Certificates of deposit, any other holdings. List how title held, beneficiaries, account number, location of property, names, addresses, phone numbers, location of holding, and agent or broker of each holding.

PERSONAL RESIDENCE AND OTHER REAL ESTATE

Address(es), Purchase date(s), Cost, How title held? (Partners? — names, addresses, phone numbers), Mortgage(s), Loan number(s) Payment(s), Due date(s), Tax parcel number(s), Homeowners and/or Mortgage insurance, Any income production?

PERSONAL

Auto(s): Year, make, model, ID number, License plate number, registration renewal date and fees, Who holds title and where kept, Name, address(es), phone number(s) of Financing or leasing institution, monthly payment(s), Warranties or extended service agreements, Service records? Who takes care of your vehicles and at what intervals? Insurance company and agent(s), Policy number(s), Who gets these vehicle(s)at death?

VALUABLES

Make a list of your valuables including furniture, machinery tools, household belongings with purchase dates and price. Include appraised value if appropriate.

Make another list of Maintenance companies and/or personnel (what they do), telephone numbers, Contract numbers. Include names and phone numbers of gardeners, repair persons, domestic help, etc.

BUSINESS

If you are self-employed then explain the details of your business and whom you want to take over in your absence. Give the name(s), address(es), phone numbers of persons to contact for help.

MISCELLANEOUS

Location and details of: Safe, Post office box, Safe deposit box, keys for various locks and/or combinations to locks, Emergency cash, Disposition of pets.

OTHER INFORMATION ABOUT HOME:

Where are the following: Heater, Water meter, Water valve for faucets, Gas meter, Main shut-off(s), Fuse boxes or Circuit breaker, Automatic sprinklers, any other information that could be useful.

PARTING WISDOM

You may want to write a letter or note to your significant other, friend(s), and/or children expressing your sentiments about your life with them. Tune into your heart with much of what you learned from doing the various processes.

APPENDIX III: HEALTH CARE DIRECTIVE The Five Wishes

An example of health care directives is included below as the Five Wishes. Check your own state for your specific directive.

To obtain a copy of an Advance Health Care Directive Kit for California, contact the CMA (California Medical Association) at 221 Main Street, P. O. Box 7690, San Francisco, CA 94120-7690.

To obtain copies of other states' Health Care Directives, contact the Medical Association in your state.

The following "Five Wishes" is a living will that is also a health directive.

FIVE WISHES®

MY WISH FOR:

The Person I Want to Make Care Decisions for Me When I Can't

The Kind of Medical Treatment I Want or Don't Want

How Comfortable I Want to Be

How I Want People to Treat Me

What I Want My Loved Ones to Know

print your name

print your birthdate

Five Wishes

There are many things in life that are out of our hands. This Five Wishes booklet gives you a way to control something very important—how you are treated if you get seriously ill. It is an easy-to-complete form that lets you say exactly what you want. Once it is filled out and properly signed it is valid under the laws of most states.

What Is Five Wishes?

Five Wishes is the first living will that talks about your personal, emotional and spiritual needs as well as your medical wishes. It lets you choose the person you want to make health care decisions for you if you are not able to make them for yourself. Five Wishes lets you say exactly how you wish to be treated if you get seriously ill. It was written with the help of The American Bar Association's Commission on the Legal Problems of the Elderly, and the nation's leading experts in end-of-life care. It's also easy to use. All you have to do is check a box, circle a direction, or write a few sentences.

How Five Wishes Can Help You And Your Family

- It lets you talk with your family, friends and doctor about how you want to be treated if you become seriously ill.
- Your family members will not have to guess what you want. It protects them if you become seriously ill, because they won't have to make hard choices without knowing your wishes.
- You can know what your mom, dad, spouse, or friend wants through a Five Wishes living will. You can be there for them when they need you most. You will understand what they really want.

How Five Wishes Began

For 12 years, a man named Jim Towey worked closely with Mother Teresa, and, for one year, he lived in a hospice she ran in Washington, DC. Inspired by this first-hand experience, Mr. Towey sought a way for patients and their families to plan ahead and to cope with serious illness. The result is Five Wishes and the response to it has been overwhelming. It has been featured on CNN and NBC's Today Show and in the pages of *Time* and *Money* magazines. Newspapers have called Five Wishes the first "living will with a heart."

2

Who Should Use Five Wishes

Five Wishes is for anyone 18 or older—married, single, parents, adult children, and friends. Over one million Americans of all ages have already used it. Because it works so well, lawyers, doctors, hospitals and hospices, churches and synagogues, employers, and retiree groups are handing out this document.

Five Wishes States

If you live in the District of Columbia or one of the 35 states listed below, you can use Five Wishes and have the peace of mind to know that it substantially meets your state's requirements under the law:

Arizona	Hawaii	Minnesota	North Dakota
Arkansas	Idaho	Mississippi	Pennsylvania
California	Illinois	Missouri	Rhode Island
Colorado	Iowa	Montana	South Dakota
Connecticut	Louisiana	Nebraska	Tennessee
Delaware	Maine	New Jersey	Virginia
District of Columbia	Maryland	New Mexico	Washington
Florida	Massachusetts	New York	West Virginia
Georgia	Michigan	North Carolina	Wyoming

If your state is not one of the 35 states listed here, Five Wishes does not meet the technical requirements in the statutes of your state. So some doctors in your state may be reluctant to honor Five Wishes. However, many people from states not on this list do complete Five Wishes along with their state's legal form. They find that Five Wishes helps them express all that they want and provides a helpful guide to family members, friends, care givers and doctors. Most doctors and health care professionals know they need to listen to your wishes no matter how you express them.

How Do I Change To Five Wishes?

You may already have a living will or a durable power of attorney for health care. If you want to use Five Wishes instead, all you need to do is fill out and sign a new Five Wishes as directed. As soon as you sign it, it takes away any advance directive you had before. To make sure the right form is used, please do the following:

- Destroy all copies of your old living will or durable power of attorney for health care. Or you can write "revoked" in large letters across the copy you have. Tell your lawyer if he or she helped prepare those old forms for you. *AND*
- Tell your Health Care Agent, family members, and doctor that you have filled out the new Five Wishes. Make sure they know about your new wishes.

3

WISH 1

The Person I Want To Make Health Care Decisions For Me When I Can't Make Them For Myself.

If I am no longer able to make my own health care decisions, this form names the person I choose to make these choices for me. This person will be my Health Care Agent (or other term that may be used in my state, such as proxy, representative, or surrogate). This person will make my health care choices if both of these things happen:

- My attending or treating doctor finds I am no longer able to make health care choices, *AND*
- Another health care professional agrees that this is true.

If my state has a different way of finding that I am not able to make health care choices, then my state's way should be followed.

The Person I Choose As My Health Care Agent Is:

First Choice Name

Phone

Address

City/State/Zip

If this person is not able or willing to make these choices for me, *OR* is divorced or legally separated from me, *OR* this person has died, then these people are my next choices:

Second Choice Name

Address

City/State/Zip

Phone

Third Choice Name

Address

City/State/Zip

Phone

Picking The Right Person To Be Your Health Care Agent

Choose someone who knows you very well, cares about you, and who can make difficult decisions. A spouse or family member may not be the best choice because they are too emotionally involved. Sometimes they are the best choice. You know best. Choose someone who is able to stand up for you so that your wishes are followed. Also, choose someone who is likely to be nearby so that they can help when you need them. Whether you choose a spouse, family member, or friend as your Health Care Agent, make sure you talk about these wishes and be sure that this person agrees to respect and follow your wishes. Your Health Care Agent should be at least 18 years or older (in Colorado, 21 years or older) and should not be:

- Your health care provider, including the owner or operator of a health or residential or community care facility serving you.
- An employee of your health care provider.
- Serving as an agent or proxy for 10 or more people unless he or she is your spouse or close relative.

4

I understand that my Health Care Agent can make health care decisions for me. I want my Agent to be able to do the following: (Please cross out anything you don't want your Agent to do that is listed below.)

- Make choices for me about my medical care or services, like tests, medicine, or surgery. This care or service could be to find out what my health problem is, or how to treat it. It can also include care to keep me alive. If the treatment or care has already started, my Health Care Agent can keep it going or have it stopped.
- Interpret any instructions I have given in this form or given in other discussions, according to my Health Care Agent's understanding of my wishes and values.
- Arrange for admission to a hospital, hospice, or nursing home for me. My Health Care Agent can hire any kind of health care worker I may need to help me or take care of me. My Agent may also fire a health care worker, if needed.
- Make the decision to request, take away or not give medical treatments, including artificially-provided food and water, and any other treatments to keep me alive.
- See and approve release of my medical records and personal files. If I need to sign my name to get any of these files, my Health Care Agent can sign it for me.
- Move me to another state to get the care I need or to carry out my wishes.
- Authorize or refuse to authorize any medication or procedure needed to help with pain.
- Take any legal action needed to carry out my wishes.
- Donate useable organs or tissues of mine as allowed by law.
- Apply for Medicare, Medicaid, or other programs or insurance benefits for me. My Health Care Agent can see my personal files, like bank records, to find out what is needed to fill out these forms.
- Listed below are any changes, additions, or limitations on my Health Care Agent's powers.

____

____

____

____

____

____

____

If I Change My Mind About Having A Health Care Agent, I Will

- Destroy all copies of this part of the Five Wishes form. *OR*
- Tell someone, such as my doctor or family, that I want to cancel or change my Health Care Agent. *OR*
- Write the word "Revoked" in large letters across the name of each agent whose authority I want to cancel. Sign my name on that page.

WISH 2

My Wish For The Kind Of Medical Treatment I Want Or Don't Want.

I believe that my life is precious and I deserve to be treated with dignity. When the time comes that I am very sick and am not able to speak for myself, I want the following wishes, and any other directions I have given to my Health Care Agent, to be respected and followed.

What You Should Keep In Mind As My Caregiver

- I do not want to be in pain. I want my doctor to give me enough medicine to relieve my pain, even if that means that I will be drowsy or sleep more than I would otherwise.
- I do not want anything done or omitted by my doctors or nurses with the intention of taking my life.
- I want to be offered food and fluids by mouth, and kept clean and warm.

What "Life-Support Treatment" Means To Me

Life-support treatment means any medical procedure, device or medication to keep me alive. Life-support treatment includes: medical devices put in me to help me breathe; food and water supplied by medical device (tube feeding); cardiopulmonary resuscitation (CPR); major surgery; blood transfusions; dialysis; antibiotics; and anything else meant to keep me alive.

If I wish to limit the meaning of life-support treatment because of my religious or personal beliefs, I write this limitation in the space below. I do this to make very clear what I want and under what conditions.

____

____

____

____

____

In Case Of An Emergency

If you have a medical emergency and ambulance personnel arrive, they may look to see if you have a Do Not Resuscitate form or bracelet. Many states require a person to have a Do Not Resuscitate form filled out and signed by a doctor. This form lets ambulance personnel know that you don't want them to use life-support treatment when you are dying. Please check with your doctor to see if you need to have a Do Not Resuscitate form filled out.

6

Here is the kind of medical treatment that I want or don't want in the four situations listed below. I want my Health Care Agent, my family, my doctors and other health care providers, my friends and all others to know these directions.

Close to death:

If my doctor and another health care professional both decide that I am likely to die within a short period of time, and life-support treatment would only delay the moment of my death (Choose *one* of the following):

❑ I want to have life-support treatment.

❑ I do not want life-support treatment. If it has been started, I want it stopped.

❑ I want to have life-support treatment if my doctor believes it could help. But I want my doctor to stop giving me life-support treatment if it is not helping my health condition or symptoms.

In A Coma And Not Expected To Wake Up Or Recover:

If my doctor and another health care professional both decide that I am in a coma from which I am not expected to wake up or recover, and I have brain damage, and life-support treatment would only delay the moment of my death (Choose *one* of the following):

❑ I want to have life-support treatment.

❑ I do not want life-support treatment. If it has been started, I want it stopped.

❑ I want to have life-support treatment if my doctor believes it could help, but I want my doctor to stop giving me life-support treatment if it is not helping my health condition or symptoms.

Permanent And Severe Brain Damage And Not Expected To Recover:

If my doctor and another health care professional both decide that I have permanent and severe brain damage, (for example, I can open my eyes, but I can not speak or understand) and I am not expected to get better, and life-support treatment would only delay the moment of my death (Choose *one* of the following):

❑ I want to have life-support treatment.

❑ I do not want life-support treatment. If it has been started, I want it stopped.

❑ I want to have life-support treatment if my doctor believes it could help. But I want my doctor to stop giving me life-support treatment if it is not helping my health condition or symptoms.

In Another Condition Under Which I Do Not Wish To Be Kept Alive:

If there is another condition under which I do not wish to have life-support treatment, I describe it below. In this condition, I believe that the costs and burdens of life-support treatment are too much and not worth the benefits to me. Therefore, in this condition, I do not want life-support treatment. (For example, you may write "end-stage condition." That means that your health has gotten worse. You are not able to take care of yourself in any way, mentally or physically. Life-support treatment will not help you recover. Please leave the space blank if you have no other condition to describe.)

____

____

____

____

____

The next three wishes deal with my personal, spiritual and emotional wishes. They are important to me. I want to be treated with dignity near the end of my life, so I would like people to do the things written in Wishes 3, 4, and 5 when they can be done. I understand that my family, my doctors and other health care providers, my friends, and others may not be able to do these things or are not required by law to do these things. I do not expect the following wishes to place new or added legal duties on my doctors or other health care providers. I also do not expect these wishes to excuse my doctor or other health care providers from giving me the proper care asked for by law.

WISH 3

My Wish For How Comfortable I Want To Be.

(Please cross out anything that you don't agree with.)

- I do not want to be in pain. I want my doctor to give me enough medicine to relieve my pain, even if that means I will be drowsy or sleep more than I would otherwise.
- If I show signs of depression, nausea, shortness of breath, or hallucinations, I want my care givers to do whatever they can to help me.
- I wish to have a cool moist cloth put on my head if I have a fever.
- I want my lips and mouth kept moist to stop dryness.
- I wish to have warm baths often. I wish to be kept fresh and clean at all times.
- I wish to be massaged with warm oils as often as I can be.
- I wish to have my favorite music played when possible until my time of death.
- I wish to have personal care like shaving, nail clipping, hair brushing, and teeth brushing, as long as they do not cause me pain or discomfort.
- I wish to have religious readings and well-loved poems read aloud when I am near death.

WISH 4

My Wish For How I Want People To Treat Me.

(Please cross out anything that you don't agree with.)

- I wish to have people with me when possible. I want someone to be with me when it seems that death may come at any time.
- I wish to have my hand held and to be talked to when possible, even if I don't seem to respond to the voice or touch of others.
- I wish to have others by my side praying for me when possible.
- I wish to have the members of my church or synagogue told that I am sick and asked to pray for me and visit me.
- I wish to be cared for with kindness and cheerfulness, and not sadness.
- I wish to have pictures of my loved ones in my room, near my bed.
- If I am not able to control my bowel or bladder functions, I wish for my clothes and bed linens to be kept clean, and for them to be changed as soon as they can be if they have been soiled.
- I want to die in my home, if that can be done.

8

WISH 5

My Wish For What I Want My Loved Ones To Know.

(Please cross out anything that you don't agree with.)

- I wish to have my family and friends know that I love them.
- I wish to be forgiven for the times I have hurt my family, friends, and others.
- I wish to have my family, friends and others know that I forgive them for when they may have hurt me in my life.
- I wish for my family and friends to know that I do not fear death itself. I think it is not the end, but a new beginning for me.
- I wish for all of my family members to make peace with each other before my death, if they can.
- I wish for my family and friends to think about what I was like before I became seriously ill. I want them to remember me in this way after my death.
- I wish for my family and friends to look at my dying as a time of personal growth for everyone, including me. This will help me live a meaningful life in my final days.
- I wish for my family and friends to get counseling if they have trouble with my death. I want memories of my life to give them joy and not sorrow.
- After my death, I would like my body to be (circle one): buried or cremated.
- My body or remains should be put in the following location________________.
- The following person knows my funeral wishes: ____________________.

If anyone asks how I want to be remembered, please say the following about me:

____

____

____

If there is to be a memorial service for me, I wish for this service to include the following (list music, songs, readings or other specific requests that you have):

____

____

____

(Please use the space below for any other wishes. For example, you may want to donate any or all parts of your body when you die. Please attach a separate sheet of paper if you need more space.)

____

____

____

9

Signing The Five Wishes Form

Please make sure you sign your Five Wishes form in the presence of the two witnesses.

I, ______________________________, ask that my family, my doctors, and other health care providers, my friends, and all others, follow my wishes as communicated by my Health Care Agent (if I have one and he or she is available), or as otherwise expressed in this form. This form becomes valid when I am unable to make decisions or speak for myself. If any part of this form cannot be legally followed, I ask that all other parts of this form be followed. I also revoke any health care advance directives I have made before.

Signature:____

Address:____

Phone:______________________________ Date:______________________

Witness Statement • (2 witnesses needed):

I, the witness, declare that the person who signed or acknowledged this form (hereafter "person") is personally known to me, that he/she signed or acknowledged this [Health Care Agent and/or Living Will form(s)] in my presence, and that he/she appears to be of sound mind and under no duress, fraud, or undue influence.

I also declare that I am over 18 years of age and am NOT:

- The individual appointed as (agent/proxy/surrogate/patient advocate/representative) by this document or his/her successor,
- The person's health care provider, including owner or operator of a health, long-term care, or other residential or community care facility serving the person,
- An employee of the person's health care provider,
- Financially responsible for the person's health care,
- An employee of a life or health insurance provider for the person,
- Related to the person by blood, marriage, or adoption, and,
- To the best of my knowledge, a creditor of the person or entitled to any part of his/her estate under a will or codicil, by operation of law.

(Some states may have fewer rules about who may be a witness. Unless you know your state's rules, please follow the above.)

Signature of Witness #1	Signature of Witness #2
Printed Name of Witness	Printed Name of Witness
Address	Address
Phone	Phone

Notarization • Only required for residents of Missouri, North Carolina, Tennessee and West Virginia

- If you live in Missouri, only your signature should be notarized.
- If you live in North Carolina, Tennessee or West Virginia, you should have your signature, and the signatures of your witnesses, notarized.

STATE OF______________________ COUNTY OF______________________

On this ____ day of ____________, 20___, the said ______________________________ ______________________, and ______________________, known to me (or satisfactorily proven) to be the person named in the foregoing instrument and witnesses, respectively, personally appeared before me, a Notary Public, within and for the State and County aforesaid, and acknowledged that they freely and voluntarily executed the same for the purposes stated therein.

My Commission Expires: ______________________________

Notary Public

10

What To Do After You Complete Five Wishes

- Make sure you sign and witness the form just the way it says in the directions. Then your Five Wishes will be legal and valid.
- Talk about your wishes with your health care agent, family members and others who care about you. Give them copies of your completed Five Wishes.
- Keep the original copy you signed in a special place in your home. Do NOT put it in a safe deposit box. Keep it nearby so that someone can find it when you need it.
- Fill out the wallet card below. Carry it with you. That way people will know where you keep your Five Wishes.
- Talk to your doctor during your next office visit. Give your doctor a copy of your Five Wishes. Make sure it is put in your medical record. Be sure your doctor understands your wishes and is willing to follow them. Ask him or her to tell other doctors who treat you to honor them.
- If you are admitted to a hospital or nursing home, take a copy of your Five Wishes with you. Ask that it be put in your medical record.
- I have given the following people copies of my completed Five Wishes:

____

____

____

Residents of Institutions In California, Connecticut, Delaware, Georgia, New York, and North Dakota Must Follow Special Witnessing Rules.

If you live in certain institutions (a nursing home, other licensed long term care facility, a home for the mentally retarded or developmentally disabled, or a mental health institution) in one of the states listed above, you may have to follow special "witnessing requirements" for your Five Wishes to be valid. For further information, please contact a social worker or patient advocate at your institution.

Five Wishes is meant to help you plan for the future. It is not meant to give you legal advice. It does not try to answer all questions about anything that could come up. Every person is different, and every situation is different. Laws change from time to time. If you have a specific question or problem, talk to a medical or legal professional for advice.

Five Wishes Wallet Card

Important Notice to Medical Personnel: I have a Five Wishes Advance Directive. ____________________ Signature Please consult this document and/or my Health Care Agent in an emergency. My Agent is: ____________________ Name ____________________ Address City/State/Zip ____________________ Phone	My primary care physician is: ____________________ Name ____________________ Address City/State/Zip ____________________ Phone My document is located at: ____________________ ____________________ ____________________ ____________________

Cut Out Card, Fold and Laminate for Safekeeping

11

Here's What People Are Saying About Five Wishes:

"It will be a year since my mother passed on. We knew what she wanted because she had the Five Wishes living will. When it came down to the end, my brother and I had no questions on what we needed to do. We had peace of mind."

Cheryl K.
Longwood, Florida

"I must say I love your Five Wishes. It's clear, easy to understand, and doesn't dwell on the concrete issues of medical care, but on the issues of real importance—human care. I used it for myself and my husband."

Susan W.
Flagstaff, Arizona

"I don't want my children to have to make the decisions I am having to make for my mother. I never knew that there were so many medical options to be considered. Thank you for such a sensitive and caring form. I can simply fill it out and have it on file for my children."

Diana W.
Hanover, Illinois

To Order:

You can order more copies of Five Wishes or the Five Wishes video—a 25-minute educational presentation that explains how to fill out Five Wishes and answers frequently asked questions. Simply call, toll-free,

1-888-5WISHES (1-888-594-7437)

Aging with Dignity

P.O. Box 1661
Tallahassee, Florida 32302-1661
www.agingwithdignity.org
1-888-594-7437

The Five Wishes project is supported by a generous grant from

The Robert Wood Johnson Foundation

Princeton, New Jersey

To Order:

You can order more copies of Five Wishes or the Five Wishes video—a 25-minute educational presentation that explains how to fill out **Five Wishes** and answers frequently asked questions. Simply call, toll-free,

1-888-5WISHES (1-888-594-7437)

Aging with Dignity

P.O. Box 1661
Tallahasse, Florida 32302-1661
www.agingwithdignity.org
1-888-594-7437

 Aging with Dignity wishes to than Oregon Health Decisions for contributing to the drafting of wish number two, and Kate Callahan for her help.

The Five Wishes project is
supported by a generous grant
from
**The Robert Wood Johnson
Foundation**
Princenton, New Jersey

BIBLIOGRAPHY : REFERENCES AND FURTHER READING

Bartholow,Jerry. *Peace Soup—The Recipe for a Peaceful Life in the New Millennium.* Birmingham, AL: PSI Publishing, 2000.

Bohm, David. *Wholeness and Implicate Order.* New York: Routledge, 2002.

Booth , Father Leo. *The God Game: It's Your Move.* Walpole, NH: Stillpoint, 1994.

—. *When God Becomes A Drug: Breaking the Chains of Religious Addiction & Abuse.* New York: Tarcher/Putnam, 1991.

Brumet, Robert. *Finding Yourself In Transition: Using Life's Changes for Spiritual Awakening.* Unity Village, MO: Unity Books, 1995.

Brussat, Frederick and Mary Ann. *Spiritual Literacy, Reading the Sacred in Everyday Life.* Chicago, IL: Touchstone, 1998.

Buber, Martin. *Tales of the Hasidim*, New York: Schocken Books, 1975.

Carroll, Lewis, et al. *Alice's Adventures in Wonderland and Through the Looking Glass.* Signet, reissue edition, 2000.

Comstock, Kani and Marisa Thame. *Journey Into Love: Ten Steps To Wholeness.* Ashland, OR: Willow Press, 2000.

Dalai Lama, His Holiness the. *How To Practice: The Way To A Meaningful Life.* New York: Pocket Books, 2002.

Dantes, Ligia. *The Unmanifest Self.* Aslan, 1990.

Dass, Ram. *Still Here, Embracing Aging, Changing, and Dying.* New York: Riverhead, 2000.

Dyer, Wayne W. *You'll See It When You Believe It: The Way To Your Personal Transformation.* Quill, 2001.

Fillmore, Charles. *The Twelve Powers Of Man*. Unity Village, MO: Unity School of Christianity, (no publishing date)

---*Christian Healing.* Unity Village, MO: Unity School of Christianity, (no publishing date)

Freeman, James Dillet. *Prayer, the Master Key.* Unity Village, MO: Unity Books, 1988.

Friedman, Norman. *Bridging Science and Spirit: Common Elements in David Bohm's Physics, The Perenial Philosophy, and Seth.* Woodbridge Group, 1998.

Funk, Robert, Ray Hoover, and The Jesus Seminar. *The Five Gospels, What Did Jesus Really Say.* Harper San Francisco, 1993.

Hanh, Thich Nhat. *The Blooming Of A Lotus: Guided Meditation Exercises For Healing And Transformation.* Boston: Beacon Press, 1993.

Harris, Rachel, Ph.D. *20-Minute Retreats.* New York: Henry Holt, 2000.

Hoffman, Bob. *Getting Divorced from Mother & Dad: The Discoveries of the Fischer-Hoffman Process.* New York: E.P. Dutton, 1976.

—. *No One Is to Blame: Freedom From Compulsive Self-Defeating Behavior.* Recycling Books, 1988.

Houff, William H. *...Infinity in Your Hand: A Guide For The Spiritually Curious.* 2nd ed. Boston, Skinner House. 1994.

Jackson, Phil. Sacred Hoops: *Spiritual Lessons of a Hardwood Warrior.* New York: Hyperion Press, 1990.

Kuritz, Martin, John Sampson, David J. Sanchez and James T. Martellaro. *The Beneficiary Book, Software for Windows.* Carlsbad, CA: Active Insights, 1996.

Kushner, Lawrence. *God Was In This Place and I Didn't Know: Finding Self, Spirituality, and Ultimate Meaning.* Woodstock, VT: Jewish Lights, 1993.

Kurtz, Ernest, and Katherine Ketcham. *The Spirituality of Imperfection: Modern Wisdom From Classic Stories.* New York: Bantam, 1992.

Levine, Stephen. *A Year To Live: How to Live This Year As If It Were Your Last.* New York: Bell Tower, 1977.

Luke, Helen M. *Kaleidoscope-The Way of Woman and Other Essays.* New York: Parabola, 1992.

Maday, Michael A. *New Thought for a New Millennium: Twelve Powers for the 21st Century.* Unity Village, MO: Unity Books, 1998.

Milton, Hal. *Going Public: A Practical Guide to Developing Personal Charisma.* Deerfield Beach, FL: Health Communications, 1995.

Moody, Harry R., Ph.D., and David Carroll. *The Five Stages Of The Soul.* Anchor, 1997.

Naranjo, Claudio, M.D. *Character and Neurosis, An Integrative View.* Nevada City: Gateways, 1994.

—. *The End Of Patriarchy And the Dawning of a Tri-une Society.* Oakland, CA: Amber Lotus, 1994.

Northrop, Christian. *Health Wisdom for Women.* New England: Newsletter, November, 2001.

Perkins-Reed, Marcia. *Thriving in Transition: Effective Living In Times Of Change.* Carmichael, CA: Touchstone Books, 1996.

Rainer, Marie Rilke. *Letters To A Young Poet.* New York: Norton, W.W. and Company, 1972.

Rumi. *Delicious Laughter, Rambunctious Teaching Stories from the Mathnawi of Jelaluddin Rumi.* Trans. Coleman Barks. Athens, GA: Maypop, 1990.

Schachter-Shalomi, Zallman and Ronald S. Miller. *From Age-ing to Sage-ing, A Profound New Vision Of Growing Older.* New York: Warner, 1995.

Spiritual Eldering Institute, 970 Aurora Avenue, Boulder, CO 80302

Stories of the Spirit, Stories of the Heart: Parables of the Spiritual Path from Around the World. Edited by Christina Feldman and Jack Kornfield. San Francisco: Harper, 1991.

The New Oxford Annotated Bible, Revised Standard Version. Oxford: Oxford UP, 1973.

Williamson, David, Gay Lynn Williamson and Robert H. Knapp. *Twelve Powers In You.* Deerfield Beach, FL: Health Communications, 2000.

ABOUT THE AUTHOR

Hal Milton's extensive background in education, athletic coaching, business and the Human Potential Movement led to a lifetime study of modalities associated with body, mind, spirit, and emotional growth. This focus prompted an integrative approach to the relationship between them. As he approaches his eighth-decade, Milton shares his unique synthesis of practical and spiritual approaches to living a full and satisfying life without regrets.

Hal Milton is an ordained Unity Minister, author, seminar leader and Certified Advanced Rolfer and Movement Teacher. He is co-minister with his wife Sonya of InsideOut Ministries, affiliated with the Association of Unity Churches and dedicated to celebrating the inherent divinity within each person.

He is the author of *Going Public: A Practical Guide to Developing Personal Charisma*.

To order a free Teacher's Guide for *Wising Up, Life Without Regrets,* or to contact the author, write:

Hal Milton

Wising Up

P.O. Box 2234

Napa, CA 94558

wisingup@sbcglobal.net

www.halmilton.com